Endorsements

With vulnerability and grace, Elizabeth shares her personal experiences of pain, loss, and redemption. For those who have struggled with the challenges that emerge when life doesn't go as intended, her story provides insight and inspiration. I recommend her book as a source of hope in the face of disappointment and as an encouraging reminder of God's steadfast love and faithfulness.
-- *Bill Buker, DMin, Ph.D., LPC*
Associate Dean and Senior Professor of Professional Counseling
Graduate School of Theology & Ministry
Oral Roberts University

Excellent! Elizabeth gives fascinating details, and her narrative style is compelling.
-- *Deron Spoo, Sr. Pastor, Author*
First Baptist Church, Tulsa, OK

A Dream Come True is one section of Elizabeth's life story. The events and experiences represent real-life encounters that many others have or will experience making this story so relatable.
-- *Kelly James, Ph.D., LPC*
National Certified Counselor

What a beautiful, heart-warming testimony to the faithfulness of God and to prayer. Thank you for sharing your story for all to hear of your life of prayer and trust, courage and obedience, love and devotion of perseverance. You have walked through trials holding God's hand all the way. Your relationship with Jesus is real - resulting in Victory!!!!

-- *Cheryl Brown*

OneHope Publishing

As I read Elizabeth's life story, I was quickly reminded of 2 Corinthians 1:3-4, "Blessed be the God and Father of our Lord Jesus Christ, the Father of mercies and the God of all comfort. He comforts us in all our affliction, so that we may be able to comfort those who are in any kind of affliction, through the comfort we receive from God." I believe this book will be a comfort to others because Elizabeth was willing to share the comfort she received from God through Christ Jesus.

-- *Richard Wilkerson*

Discipleship Group Leader

First Baptist Church, Tulsa

A Dream Come True

Finding Unwavering Faith

Elizabeth Howell

Written by Elizabeth Howell

PUBLISHED BY THE HOWELL GROUP - TULSA

Printed by Kindle Direct Publishing, an Amazon.com Company

Cover Design by Berge Design

ISBN: 9798392401093

Printed in the United States of America

2023 – First Edition

Acknowledgments

"Every book takes a journey" is a quote I read from one of Louie Guilo's books and I couldn't agree more! I'm indebted to a host of people who invested their time and energy into making this book *A Dream Come True,* a reality.

I give thanks to my dear friend Elizabeth Wietholter who assisted with shaping the story, proofreading, editing, and continual encouragement. To Pat Woodrum who complimented me when she offered to read, comment, and edit the book.

Judy Giles, my best friend, knows my heart and is always available to listen to new ideas, read first drafts, and cheer me on to the finish line even when I wasn't sure if I could make it!

Friends, Mike, and Cheryl Brown of OneHope Publishing, for their guidance and confirmation that I could self-publish! I had prayed and asked God what I should do regarding publishing and then ran into Cheryl the following day. We had a delightful and encouraging conversation and with it my answer.

Andrea Lende of Beatitudes Publishing LLC, a miracle received in the home stretch. Learning beside her about how to create searchable content that would help reach a wide audience. Working with me until the last possible moment, to make the book all it could be and directing me through the maze of self-publishing on KDP.

To my friends who took the time to read the drafts, and support my efforts, thank you. I appreciate your support, thoughts, and ideas; Marcel Corby, Cheryl Brown, Beverly Allan, Sally Taggert, Debbie Nomura, Bill Buker, Kelly James, Deron Spoo, and Richardson Wilkerson.

To my favorite children, Catie and Elliott, now, young adults you have my heart and I love you more than you will ever realize. What an honor it is to be your Mom. I am proud of the people you are becoming and look forward to being in your bright future.

My husband Joe, you walked the journey with me and stood by my side. Thank you.

I am forever grateful for my God and Savior Jesus Christ. This journey of life we are all experiencing is only possible with you at the helm. Thank you for loving us and dying on the cross so that we may have eternal life. We are children of the Most High God robed in righteous and made in your image. This book would not have been possible if I had not taken this journey, and through it, you NEVER left my side, even though there were times I wondered if I could make it. As I wrote this book, the miracles received were outstanding gifts from God. Every single one. Thank you for challenging me to share my heart so that others can read and experience, through my story, the gifts you have for each one of us.

Dedication

I dedicate this book to my Mom, Florence Leaver,
you were taken too early in my life and I know
the prayers and petitions voiced on my behalf
have made me become the person I am today.
I miss you dearly and thank you.

Forward

When I began writing *"A Dream Come True"* I was in the midst of one of the hardest journeys in my life. The storm was outrageous, severe, and violent. The intense winds seemed to come out of nowhere at times, strong and forceful, ripping my soul into shreds, robbing me of any hope and I began to question who I really was and if I could make it back to my core.

Being in that state, as I wrote, recalling and reliving the events of my life, God brought to my mind, whispering His reminders of how faithful and consistent He was during those times. He shared that the desires of my heart were never thrown to the wind, never unimportant, just not in my timing or by my methods. God showered me again with His power and loving truth that as I walked through my current darkness His light shinned on me in the past and will do so again.

It has been through those experiences when I was on the brink of devastation that God showed me how good He is and how very much He loves me and never leaves my side. I am never alone. Even if I felt helpless, I never was. He was right beside me carrying me, dabbing my sores with His healing balm, and restoring my dry parched soul with living water.

I've often struggled with how hard life is and asked God, "Why have you called me to handle the hard, the unusual? Why can't I walk through this life and be asked to do easier things?"

As my life journey has ensued, and I'm still standing, it has become evident that God has given me the strength to continue moving forward, to pursue when others would give up, to continue searching for Him, and not stop until I find Him. To pick up the pieces of a shredded life and know that as I walk through the valley of the shadow of death, I don't need to fear, because God is right beside me. We serve an enormous, loving, faithful, and caring God who wants the best for us. Although the memories on these pages are a few of my life's experiences, my hope is that through them you too will encounter the hope and true love that is available to us all through Jesus Christ.

Speaker | Story Teller | Author - Booking Opportunities contact -
TheHowellGroupTulsa@gmail.com

Table of Contents

PART I: THE LONGING

Chapter 1 – The Beginning

The ticking of the clock seemed to add time instead of reducing it. Why was it that watching the numbers change from one to two seemed to take so long? Would Elizabeth receive the answer she desired?

Three minutes passed, which seemed like an hour. When would the results appear?

The dream of becoming a Mom was in Elizabeth's heart and mind. She knew she was already late to try, and her internal clock was ticking. Having struggled just to keep her reproductive organs, Elizabeth clung to her dream. She married in her thirties, with forty on the horizon. She knew she needed to talk with her husband Joe about children. Communication was challenging during their courtship, and that pattern carried over into their marriage.

Both had demanding careers and focused on them. They had been married for six years, and Elizabeth was ready to resign from her corporate position and fulfill her dream. The accolades, acknowledgments, and salary of her current position had helped distract her heart, but it wasn't the solution. A dangling carrot that

1

kept her focused, determined, and unstoppable, even to the detriment of her health. She loved her job and yet the dream of becoming a Mom was that which activated her heart.

Elizabeth's desire to become a Mom came from being loved by a nurturing, caring Mother herself. Growing up in a family of five boys and one girl, the females stayed together. That bonded them. Her Mother's motto was - "serve others, be kind, and love Jesus". Their relationship had been just too short, only fifteen years together stolen too quickly, Elizabeth cherished her memories. Knowing someone had your back, would be there, and understood you, was very reassuring for her. She missed her Mom so much. There were too many of Elizabeth's life experiences that were never shared with her Mom. She had left this earth too soon.

When Elizabeth married Joe, getting pregnant was never a thought that crossed her mind. She and Joe had a rousing chemistry. During their eight years of on and off again dating, there were times they needed to chill a little bit. So, when Elizabeth and Joe started trying to become pregnant it didn't surprise her how soon after that the results seemed to come.

Purchasing a pregnancy test and taking it caused Elizabeth's stomach to jump up and down. She paced in the bathroom, wearing the tile floor out waiting for the results. Afraid to look at the test stick, she didn't want to be disappointed, and yet she couldn't wait to see the little bright red line appearing, meaning she was pregnant.

After three minutes, which seemed like forever, the bright red line appeared, and tears began to slowly stream down Elizabeth's face. Her thoughts went from thrilled to ecstatic. The joy was overflowing. As tears flooded her face, thoughts of Elizabeth's Mom rushed to her heart. The tenderness her Mom continually shared with Elizabeth was something so dear and intensely missed. Sharing this experience with her Mom was a longing Elizabeth had deep within her heart and yet, it would never happen.

The activities of the day continued and when Elizabeth saw Joe, she shared the news. Elizabeth was upbeat and excited. Joe was happy but reserved in his response. It was Friday night and hitting golf balls was a regular activity. Walking down to the field to set up for the first practice round, Elizabeth began to feel uneasy, her stomach and back began to ache. Not knowing how to take this physical response regarding the wonderful news, Elizabeth was concerned. But she didn't share her concern with Joe right away.

As the evening progressed, the pain intensified to full-on cramps. *"No,"* Elizabeth thought, *"please don't let anything go wrong"*. Continuing to hit golf balls, but becoming more withdrawn with the process, Elizabeth's thoughts turned to losing the baby she was carrying inside her womb.

The time at the driving range seemed to drag on. Joe noticed Elizabeth wasn't quite into her swing like she usually was and quieter than normal.

Once at home preparing a quick dinner, Elizabeth started spotting and tried to will the cramps away. The physical pain was uncomfortable, even though she was no stranger to intense and severe cramps. She finally broke down and told Joe about the pain she was experiencing inside her womb. He listened, while she shared, with a longing in his eyes. His hug communicated his reassurance to her that he was with her, as best as he could be.

Elizabeth hated to even admit out loud that she was experiencing painful cramps. Her heart was so heavy, and she just wanted to cry. But Joe suggested a movie to turn the focus off of the obvious.

In the middle of the night, Elizabeth was awakened with excruciatingly painful cramps. Lying in bed, tossing and turning, she just couldn't get comfortable, the pain became worse. Joe was snoring soundly, and she didn't want to wake him. She felt so bad. What was happening? Surely it couldn't be. Not being able to stay in bed any longer, Elizabeth got up and went into the bathroom.

4

Her feet beneath her felt like rocks. She could barely pick them up to walk to the bathroom. Her legs were throbbing with pain. Her entire lower pelvic area was cramping hard. The toilet seemed miles away. Upon reaching it she sat down, and a gush of clotted brown blood was released from Elizabeth's body. She burst into tears and wanted to scream. *"No, it just can't be. I had prayed so hard for a child."* Elizabeth's heavy heart was shrieking. She couldn't believe what had happened. Losing the baby just as fast as they had made him/her.

Her heart was broken in two. Sobbing came in crashing waves and yet she felt a peace that was amazing to feel, the peace that only God could bring to her heart. She was losing her son or daughter and still was praising God. Singing the old hymns she had sung with her Mom when she was young. Maybe it was God's way of bringing Elizabeth's Mom to the experience. It was odd, Elizabeth was losing a dream right before her eyes, and yet singing hymns and thinking about her Mom brought such joy to her heart. She asked God, "What's next, Lord? You know my heart. Will my dream ever come true?"

Somehow Elizabeth was able to return to bed, the walk was slow, and it seemed like miles away, still cramping but nothing like earlier. Elizabeth felt so empty inside. Their child was no longer growing in her womb and a deep sadness enveloped all around her.

Monday morning came and with it, another day at work. Elizabeth felt numb, but the responsibilities of the day found her hosting an executive from out of town. Being numb wasn't an option. Putting on the "career-woman persona" and meeting the objective of the day was a must. Elizabeth drew a breath and thought, "I'll just suck it up and move forward." This attitude always worked, and she'd use it to just push through the pain. But even her best survival techniques wouldn't budge the thoughts and heartache of what had just happened; they were so fresh and painful.

Joe and Elizabeth typically kept to themselves about their lives. Alone with her feelings when Marlene, Elizabeth's cousin, called the following day and shared about her friend's daughter getting pregnant. Listening to the story wasn't easy. The young daughter had decided to give her baby up for adoption. Elizabeth thought the timing of the conversation was interesting, but still didn't share about her loss. She didn't want to say it out loud, for that made it too real. After the conversation ended, Elizabeth took a shower and once inside the sobs didn't stop. She couldn't control them. Feeling the water cascade over her body, it carried the sobs filled with heartbreak, pain, and emptiness down the drain. She prayed that she could get pregnant, carry the baby to term and live her heart's desire, to be a Mom.

Joe went with Elizabeth to her doctor's appointment the following week. Her physical body had recovered, and the doctor didn't feel surgery was necessary. As the appointment continued, Joe and Elizabeth were ushered into the doctor's office. Trying to use words of comfort, the doctor shared the statistics. Seventy-five percent of all first pregnancies end in miscarriage. Elizabeth didn't really hear much of what was said. It was too much to process, plus it wasn't what she wanted to hear. Losing her first baby just as fast as making it wasn't right wasn't fair. Elizabeth wanted to be in the twenty-five percent of the statistics, not the seventy-five percent.

Resuming life after being pregnant was not an easy transition. Returning to work and filling the hole in her heart wasn't simple. The devices she had fallen back on in painful situations before, just weren't working. Work wasn't as exciting anymore. The old daily routines and structure didn't keep Elizabeth's mind from wandering. Her heart was empty, broken, and hollow and she didn't know how to fix it.

As Elizabeth reflected, she and Joe had taken it for granted that they would have children and it wouldn't be hard. The process wouldn't be drawn out and there wouldn't be so much heartache. Her Mother had had six children, sometimes planned pregnancies and others not. Elizabeth picked up her Bible and searched for comfort. Landing in her favorite book, Psalms, she found verses that touched her heart.

Delight yourself in the Lord and he will give you the desires of your heart. He will make your righteousness shine like the dawn. Be still before the Lord and wait patiently for him. Psalm 37:4-7

The feelings of pain and loss were not new to Elizabeth. She found strength from the words she had just read. *"So, Lord, if I put those words into action. If I delight myself in you, follow you with every fiber of my being, you'll give me the desires of my heart, which is to be a Mom?"*

She felt a sense of peace and an answer. *The "be still before the Lord and wait patiently for Him"* was going to be more of a stretch. Elizabeth was a problem solver. Identify the problem, decide on a solution, and then implement it. Being still wasn't one of her strongest qualities, nor was patience; these two areas definitely needed work.

A vacation trip East was on the schedule for Joe and Elizabeth that year. Driving to Highlands, North Carolina gave them time to enjoy the beautiful landscape that God created and time together. Five days at High Hampton Resort, a favorite mountain retreat, removed from the hustle and bustle, but not remote, social but not stuffy, charming, and historical. This time away proved relaxing and enjoyable. As it rained one evening, Joe and Elizabeth rocked in the rocking chairs on the porch just off their room, enjoying the sound of the rain hitting the leaves on the trees, and smelling the fresh clean mountain air. They held hands and focused on just being quiet together.

Many activities were offered at the resort, although the countryside called to Joe's heart. The greenery and lushness of the rural area were breathtaking. It was during this trip that Joe explained to Elizabeth about the aggressive plant called, Kudzu. It was everywhere, a trailing perennial vine native to East Asia and Southeast Asia and invasive in North America. Joe shared that it was introduced from Japan to the United States as an ornamental and forage crop plant. The Civilian Conservation Corps and southern farmers planted kudzu to control soil erosion. The vine climbs, coils around, and smothers any living thing that it grows on. Death is slow to the other plants as the Kudzu hogs all the sunlight and eventually suffocates the plants and trees.

Elizabeth began experiencing intense cramps again and the loss of their baby was at the forefront of her mind. The smothering concept of the kudzu plant correlated to the feelings in her heart, suffocating her dream. She needed to focus on the positive and not allow the sadness to take over. She had so much to be thankful for her good health, work, husband, and friends that made her laugh

9

and love. Joe tried to be accommodating and kind, aware of Elizabeth's physical and emotional pain. But the reach wasn't quite making it to her burdened, heavy heart.

Elizabeth continued to reflect on the promises of God. She knew He was right beside her, yet she still couldn't understand why it had happened. She wanted to be faithful to God and lean into Him. She found scripture, which she held onto. Over and over, she heard *"I am with you, neither death nor life, neither spirit-powers present nor future fears, height, depth, not ANYTHING else in all creation will separate you from My love."* Walking this out was going to take time, and God was the only one who could carry her through this valley.

On to Toledo, Ohio, they visited the Zoo. Walking around the zoo seeing the amazing exhibits and lush landscape features while holding hands was fun, the scenery was inviting. They embraced it and ate lunch at the park. The hot dog tasted good. As they ate, they noticed families and individual children in the area interacting with the animals, laughing, yelling, and expressing their excitement, Joe and Elizabeth took it all in.

Just being together helped Elizabeth's heart. Focusing on quiet meals, embracing one another, and having simple conversations were building blocks for not only a great vacation but strengthening their marriage as well. Joe loved exploring each

10

city's landscape and unique topography. Elizabeth just enjoyed being with Joe, seeing the beauty around them was icing on the cake.

From Toledo, they were off to Chicago for a White Sox baseball game, and time spent with Elizabeth's brother Mike and his wife Susie rounded off the vacation. Sadly, a treacherous rainstorm came on the night of the baseball game. In minutes, they were drenched, including their food. Nothing was shared about what Elizabeth had experienced. She wanted to move forward, not reflect on the past, even though her heart was heavy and the surges of pain within her ached.

Back home from the vacation, Joe and Elizabeth had to face reality. Their work often kept them apart both physically and emotionally. But their work defined them and that's how it always was.

Elizabeth dug deep into her work. She made a lateral change in her position to fill the desire for a new challenge. Then another opportunity for a Directorship was offered, which provided a salary increase, with a different bonus structure, and more responsibility, which demanded additional time at the office. Success came. Her team continued to grow and met the team's annual objectives, which affirmed her abilities as a leader.

The stress experienced with the Directorship manifested itself through Elizabeth's health, mouth ulcers, and lack of sleep. Her mind never seemed to slow down and stop. Even on weekends, work was a priority either at the office or working from home. Joe found himself in the same position. Having recently started a new consulting firm, his focus was on growing and building his business. Work was something they both knew well, and it had previously brought comfort and satisfaction. It defined and affirmed who they were as individuals and now as a couple.

Through all the career movement and momentum, the emptiness in Elizabeth's heart wasn't going away. She prayed for the desire of her heart, the ability to be still and be patient, and knew somehow, someway, it would come to fruition. But she also knew she wasn't getting any younger.

When and how was it going to happen?

--TAKE AWAY--

- God hears every single prayer we pray, even when we don't see the evidence or answer we want.

1 John 5:14 *"And we are confident that he hears us whenever we ask for anything that pleases him. And since we know He hears us when we make our requests, we also know He will give us what we ask for."*

Romans 8:28 *"And we know that God causes everything to work together for the good of those who love God and are called according to his purpose for them."*

God understands and knows the desires in our hearts. Petitioning and pouring your heart out to God is exactly what we need to do. Waiting for the answer isn't easy, at times it's very hard, but we will always receive an answer either, Yes, No, wait, or not yet.

When our prayers seem to go unanswered, we may feel we are walking through the valley of the shadow of death. Day after day, you lift your petitions to God, and the answer doesn't come. God never stops working on your behalf. He is orchestrating what and whom He needs to be put in place, so when the time is right His answer is evident. On those days when the answers don't come as quickly, rejoice in knowing God is working on your behalf. He knows exactly what is best for you in every situation.

- God never leaves us or forsakes us.

Joshua 1:9 *"Have I not commanded you? Be strong and courageous. Do not be frightened, and do not be dismayed, for the Lord your God is with YOU wherever you go."*

Isaiah 41:10 *"Fear not, for I am with you; be not dismayed, for I am our God, I will strengthen you, I will help you, I will uphold you with my righteous right hand."*

Sometimes we are the ones that move – in attitude, actions, or belief. God is continually working on our behalf. So often as we walk the journey out, if we knew what was entailed and how long, intense and exhausting it would be, we would turn around and run and miss the blessing He has waiting for us to receive.

Standing on the word of God, saying it out loud, breathing, believing, and living it is the only way to get through tough times.

Hebrews 4:12 *"For the word of God is living and active, sharper than any two-edged sword, piercing to the division of soul and of spirit, of joints and of marrow, and discerning the thoughts and intentions of the heart."*

Psalm 18:30 *"This God – His way is perfect; the word of the Lord proves true; He is a shield for all those who take refuge in Him."*

God's truth, His word, is the only anchor in this life we are living today. We can claim its promises morning, noon, and night. And tomorrow they will be the same. Choose to claim the victories and turn your thoughts in another direction – God's direction. Christ's strength moves in our weakness.

Live in the light of truth. Our Holy Savior is the Light of the World. Focus on whose you are – not on who you are or the circumstances that you are experiencing. Remember you are a child of the King who is robed in righteousness.

A DREAM COME TRUE

Chapter 2 – Say It Isn't So

Traveling for work from coast to coast had become routine. Elizabeth worked non-stop, carrying around the emptiness in her heart. She tried to suppress the feelings to keep them as low as they would go, and yet, they still seemed to surface under the oddest of circumstances. Her mind would wander and ask, *"When will this stop?"* The real question she was thinking was, *"When would she become pregnant and begin living her dream?"*

Asking God questions wasn't something Elizabeth did often. When the feelings arose in her heart and her throat experienced tightness to keep them at bay she would dismiss them.

Her success as a Director wasn't holding the same level of stimulation and challenge as it once did. She enjoyed various aspects of the position, but leading the team could either bring success or misery. Elizabeth began experiencing mouth ulcers, which caused agonizing pain. The more stress she was under, the worse the pulsating of the ulcers became. Trying to get rid of the pain no matter what medication, vitamin, or procedure tried just wasn't happening. The sores weren't going anywhere and increased in size. Being frustrated and in continual pain, she pushed through the workload that needed to be completed ... She wasn't a failure.

Elizabeth's best friend, Judy, worked as a Director also, they were promoted to their positions within the same timeframe. Judy provided directorship for the Account Managers, while Elizabeth directed the Account Executives. They had worked together for the last eight years, both hired as Account Executives and then promoted through the ranks, accepting challenges and opportunities which stretched them mentally and physically.

When Judy and Elizabeth were hired, three other Account Executives were also. The company needed a team to implement its latest software products. The five Account Executives became known as the "Fearless Five", their success affected the company's ranking within the industry and provided a solid foundation for their careers.

Judy differed from any of the other Account Executives hired. Her heart was tender, kind, and full of grace. Everyone gravitated to her friendliness. Her light radiated from within, no matter the situation or what she accomplished. Her humility was noteworthy and reflective. And Elizabeth knew there was something different about her.

If either of them needed help, if the other was available, they always helped each other no matter what they had to do. When first hired, Judy needed help with the operating system the software ran on. Elizabeth would come in early to work and

18

provide training for Judy so she could operate the software without a hitch. Whenever they could travel to the same city together to install a software system, they did.

Laughing, crying, and sharing their hearts, they built a friendship that was honest, true, and never taken for granted. Judy knew Jesus, and the evidence of that relationship was expressed whenever she interacted with others. Elizabeth looked up to Judy. She admired her. Judy's positivity was infectious, yet when she struggled due to issues outside her control, she would paddle like a fast and furious duck. But she always managed to stay calm on the surface.

After being promoted to Director, some of the travel lessened and they officed out of the corporate location. They went to lunch together as often as their schedule allowed and stepped into each other's office for a quick chat or to check in every morning. Judy naturally reflected a warm and engaging response, which brightened Elizabeth's day before the workday started.

Elizabeth had met Jesus in a miraculous way, but her relationship with Him wasn't as obvious. Her focus was more on herself than on others. Elizabeth kept to herself, was kind to others, and completed her work with intensity, but did not gravitate to other team members but Judy. The Account Executives would socialize outside the office regularly and Judy and Elizabeth were often asked, but usually didn't join them.

Sharon, one of the other Account Executives, was always jealous of Elizabeth's success. It felt like Sharon sabotaged people or incidents to negatively impact Elizabeth. Not knowing where to turn, Elizabeth would pray for wisdom and guidance regarding Sharon. As the situation escalated, Elizabeth became frustrated and turned to Judy for a listening ear.

At times, not having a college degree made Elizabeth feel inadequate, and she pushed through harder to prove she could complete what was asked of her. Judy listened as Elizabeth shared with her and affirmed that she also saw things Sharon did. She suggested that the two of them begin praying together on their lunch break, and that's what they did. Elizabeth hadn't really prayed for her enemies so specifically before, in fact, she couldn't remember if she ever had prayed for her enemies. Now as she did, God lightened her heart as she shared her concerns, fears, and worries about Sharon with Him.

And in time, it worked!

Elizabeth saw that Sharon's actions weren't about her but how Sharon saw herself.

Time moved forward, and Elizabeth's heart grew weary regarding her Directorship. She and Joe talked about her resigning and joining him at his firm, with the goal of becoming pregnant. She welcomed the opportunity of allowing her body to rest, so she could become more relaxed with less tension and stress. They set the plan in place, and Elizabeth gave a six-week notice.

As Elizabeth prepared for the big day, she didn't know what to expect. Her job was who she was. Without it, what would she fall back on? Who would Elizabeth be? The day came, the farewell party happened, and Elizabeth worked until 6:00 p.m. Leaving was harder than she had ever imagined. The desire to leave things in good shape was her focus. She generated reports, filed files, and updated policies and procedures before she knew it, it was time to walk out the door. An odd feeling came over her, knowing she wouldn't be returning to a company she had given the last ten years of her life.

And then, it hit her, what was she walking into?

Working at a six-person firm differed from a corporate environment. Elizabeth was used to standards, policies, and procedures, and many more people to interact with. Entering Joe's firm, she was the only female, and *"the wife"* as well. The realization sank in that this was going to take some getting used to, for everyone, especially Elizabeth.

21

As their plan moved forward, Joe and Elizabeth decided to both get tested to verify they could have children. Additional testing and medicines were undertaken, and the process began over several months.

In late fall, Elizabeth took another pregnancy test. Waiting with anticipation, but not as intense as the first time, the bright red line appeared on the stick meaning she was pregnant. Exhilaration came over Elizabeth and her heart leaped with joy. Sharing the news with Joe, he smiled but remained apprehensive about how her body would handle the pregnancy.

Elizabeth told no one. She was fearful if shared so early and something happened, she would have a harder time disclosing the outcome. Thoughts of repeating that loss all over again were just too hard to face.

The morning sickness started about six weeks into the pregnancy and Elizabeth thanked God during those nauseous periods of the day. Eating small amounts of food multiple times a day and drinking water seemed to help some. She also found that drinking anything containing ginger in it also helped. Her thoughts would often trail to a prayer, *"God hear my cry, and give me my heart's desire. Thank you. Please, Lord, allow our baby to grow and develop to be strong and courageous as your word states."*

Knowing a child was growing in her womb Elizabeth felt complete, warm, fulfilled, and special, oh so very special. The first three months Elizabeth felt like she was on an amusement ride that would never end. The morning sickness continued and got to where she never knew when she'd feel bad or good.

In her fourth month, the morning sickness stopped, and Elizabeth became concerned. Had it just stopped? Or was something wrong? Elizabeth's heart sank and fear set in. Her thoughts contradicted themselves. *"Stand firm, God answered your prayer with a child that is growing in your womb."* Then Satan would whisper all-knowing like, *"You'll probably lose this baby as well."* Will I ever carry a child to full-term? Why is this happening? *Lord, help me please*, Elizabeth pleaded.

She let a few days pass before she made a doctor's appointment and willed for the morning sickness to return. Sadly, telling the nurse why she needed an appointment, she expressed a long-drawn-out sigh. Here we go again. Telling Joe that evening, he shared with her he was sorry and that they wouldn't know anything until after she went to the doctor. Not receiving more emotional support took a toll on Elizabeth's feelings and mood. She needed Joe to empathize with her. Her heart was so heavy, and she needed more assurance than what she received. She kept her feelings inside. She had become a pro at doing that. Just push them down and they'll go away.

23

At the doctor's appointment, they whisked her away for blood tests first, then an ultra-sound. Elizabeth asked the nurse if she could see the ultrasound monitor, but the nurse seemed to ignore her request. Elizabeth's heart was so heavy and burdened. She hadn't asked Joe to go with her, and he didn't offer. She wanted to be anywhere but in the doctor's office, waiting for an answer she didn't want to hear. The doctor came in and shared the news, direct and to the point, that there wasn't a baby in her womb any longer and that he wanted to schedule a D&C in the next couple of days. It was all so sterile and routine, tears streamed down Elizabeth's face, and she couldn't wait to get out of there.

With no smiles or interaction with anyone, Elizabeth fled the office. She wanted to be alone. To cry until there were no more tears, by herself grieving for the child she wanted so badly. She wanted her Mom to hold her, wipe her tears, and tell her everything was going to be okay, even if it wasn't. How she longed for her Mom. Elizabeth knew she would understand and empathize with her. Cry tears of loss and just hold her tightly. She needed that so badly.

Elizabeth's thoughts drifted to when her Mom was alive. Forty-three was just too young to die. Brain cancer was an ugly death and Elizabeth was so thankful for the last couple of years with her Mom. During that time words and feelings were never hard to share. Her Mom shared from her heart her dreams for her daughter.

Feeling so overwhelmed and not knowing where to turn, Elizabeth could barely drive home, but somehow, she got there. After she composed herself, she returned to work.

Joe was in his office, and she went in and told him. He was concerned for Elizabeth and told her how apprehensive he was about her carrying the baby. All Elizabeth heard was that he didn't think she could carry a baby. The waves of a hurricane seemed to rock Elizabeth's heart, *"Why would that be the only thing she heard Joe say? Is he so far removed, that he couldn't see her falling apart? Is it that work is so important and that's his main focus, he can't see beyond it?"*

A thirst for answers consumed her, like a person wandering in the desert. The flames burning deep within her heart and mind engulfed her. Why? How? Will it ever happen? What did I do wrong? The arrows and accusations didn't stop. She felt like such a failure, empty, angry, and overwhelmed.

In her career, success had come to Elizabeth because she was focused, hard-working, and never stopped until the challenge was met. She stayed the course no matter what the toll on her physically, mentally, or emotionally. She was driven to the core.

And here she was, the second baby conceived and nurtured through good food, rest, music, and loving prayerful thoughts and they still die, without acknowledgment that they once lived. This just couldn't be. Why couldn't Elizabeth carry a baby? Why couldn't the desire of her heart be fulfilled? The feelings of failure, being crushed and beaten, encroached Elizabeth's heart and wouldn't leave. She didn't want to live, and the desire in her heart for her husband to understand and empathize was too much to bear.

So lonely, and nowhere to turn day after day, night after night, how long could this go on? Joe wanted to comfort her, and he tried, but the way he chose to comfort her wasn't what Elizabeth needed or understood. A deeper emotional connection was something that they didn't experience in their marriage. Tears poured out on her pillow at night and stung her throat during the day.

Through it all, Elizabeth got up every day and went to work.

Our bodies are uniquely and wonderfully made. It is a scientific fact that when we are afraid or traumatized, the body activates its sympathetic nervous system. The heart races, breathing becomes faster and shallower and our muscles tense up. So, we run to our non-anxious presence, our comfort or protector.

After fifteen, Elizabeth didn't have that option. Her Mom was gone, her father didn't show up and her husband didn't know how. The only one Elizabeth could run to was God. God loved her so much that He sent his only son to die for her. Even if she were the only one, He would have still sent his son to die for her. God's love pierces through any poisonous arrow that is flung. God's love is and was the answer.

Finally calling out to God, pleading with Him to give her hope, any hope, just something to cling to as she walked this journey alone, she picked up the Bible and searched for comfort. First, the Psalms, then Isaiah, and then the verses jumped off the pages, she found God's answer, just what she needed.

"Have you never heard?

Have you never understood?

The Lord is the everlasting God

The Creator of all the earth

He never grows weak or weary

No one can measure the depths of His understanding

He gives power to the weak and

He gives strength to the powerless

Even youths will become weak and tired

And young men will fall in exhaustion

But those who trust in the Lord, will find new strength

They will soar high on wings like eagles

They will run and not grow weary.

They will walk and not faint." Isaiah 40:28-31

Elizabeth wanted to soar high on God's wings. The desire to walk and not faint was very intense. She wanted strength to go on and longed to reconnect with Joe on an emotional level. Losing another baby brought up the grief from the first miscarriage and the loss of her Mom. Keeping the grief pushed down took so much energy that she didn't have.

Clinging to the verses she just found, Elizabeth fought the fight to stay the course, to believe that God was in total control, and to trust Him with everything. Every tear, sigh, and thought of confusion. Every hurt feeling and message Satan brought up to taunt her.

Six weeks later, Elizabeth ran into a good friend of hers, Elizabeth W., and she asked how she and Joe were doing. During their time together, adoption wove its way into the conversation and Elizabeth W. shared the experience she and her husband had with both of their adoptions. Having used different organizations, they experienced both a closed and open adoption. Elizabeth listened with an open heart, but her true desire was to carry a child in her womb. Open adoption sounded challenging and Elizabeth W.'s encounter proved to stretch not only her faith but also who she was as a person.

Elizabeth went home and researched the concept of open adoption. The research stated that since the 1970's it was found that open adoption was better for the adopted child. The tide was changing and by the early 1990's open adoptions were offered by a majority of American adoption agencies.

Simply stated, open adoption allows birth parents to know and have contact with the adoptive family. Birth mothers are given the option to choose a family to raise their child. They can talk with them, meet them in person, and include them in the experience at the hospital when the baby is born.

Elizabeth let the research resonate in her heart. If this were the avenue that God had for her and Joe to become a family, could she do it? Could they do it?

-- TAKE AWAY—

- Working hard like Martha without a Mary Spirit can lead to a dead end.

Luke 10:41-42 "But the Lord said to her, my dear Martha, you are worried and upset over all these details. There is only one thing worth being concerned about Mary has discovered it and it will not be taken away from her."

We must remember that we do not have to work to earn eternity. We must repent and give everything to God and not try to work harder, stronger, or longer – but release and give control to Christ. Martha worked so very hard to prepare a meal for her Lord and became upset when Mary just sat with Jesus, but Mary stood still and listened to Jesus.

Our task-oriented soul can take our intentions of doing something right in the wrong direction and cause us to end up in the wrong place. The spirit behind our responses to Christ makes all the difference. We must choose to surrender to Christ all of our worries, concerns, and anxieties, lean on Him, and believe His word. Carry it with you wherever you go and meditate on it day and night. God's kingdom can NEVER be shaken. Rest in Him.

- Stand firm on God's promises.

Isaiah 41:10 "So do not fear, I am with you, do not be dismayed, for I am your God, I will strengthen you and help you, I will uphold you with my righteous right hand."

Isaiah 26:3 "You will keep in perfect peace those whose minds are steadfast, because they trust in you."

Deuteronomy 31:8 "The Lord himself goes before you and will be with you; he will never leave you or forsake you. Do not be afraid; do not be discouraged."

God's promises are powerful tools. Equip yourself with them. God will never delay His promise. His power is made perfect in our weakness. Those who hope in the Lord will renew their strength. They will soar high on wings like eagles; they will run and not grow weary, they will walk and not faint.

A DREAM COME TRUE

PART II: RECEIVING THE GIFT

Chapter 3 – Follow Me and Be Obedient

Settling into Joe's firm was a real change, and Elizabeth learned the operations of the firm with ease. Managing the day-to-day operational functions was undemanding compared to her last position.

The inevitable question continued to rise in Elizabeth's thoughts the longer she worked for Joe. Working downtown, she would seldom see children with their parents, but looking out the large picture window in her office, longing to hold a baby in her arms, she would draw a picture in her mind of them strolling through the courtyard across the street.

If Elizabeth contacted the adoption agency to begin the process, what would happen? Were she and Joe suitable? What would they ask? Would anyone pick them? Were they too old? Joe was 45 and Elizabeth was 39. Did they work too much? What would the agency be looking for?

Sometimes Elizabeth allowed her thoughts to drift off to adoption. She was open to considering this, but not sure of the process. Joe was open, and he took a passive position of going with the flow. He knew Elizabeth's desire to have children and supported her. But it would be Elizabeth who would need to take the first step.

The day came and Elizabeth contacted the agency her friends had used. The first step on the list was to meet with the Executive Director, Laurie Jackson. Questions filled Elizabeth's head again. *"Would Laurie like them? Did they fit the profile? Would this work? Was this cost prohibitive?"*

Laurie was a delight and answered all of Elizabeth and Joe's questions. She explained the process and the history of the Adoption Agency, founded on the principle of providing women with an alternative choice for their baby. They provided support at a very vulnerable time in women's lives. Their support was through love and nurturing them to grow and assist with a plan for parenting or an adoption plan for their child.

It surprised Elizabeth to learn that she even had a relationship with the church that sponsored the agency. During a rather difficult time earlier in her life, Elizabeth attended the church. It was an inviting environment, the people were open and caring, and Elizabeth enjoyed the pastor's radio program, which she had listened to often.

Joe and Elizabeth left with a better understanding of the open adoption process and a to-do list. The adoption application was quite lengthy, and they needed a list to complete all of the requirements. Pull financial statements, write a personal biography about each of themselves, obtain personal character references, complete background checks, acquire a medical update, and complete a home study conducted by a social worker. Another daunting task, which was part of the application, was to create a Life Book, which told the story of Joe and Elizabeth's life and of how a baby would fit into their world.

The process to complete all the requirements in a timely manner was at first a real stretch for both Elizabeth and Joe. Jumping in with both feet, Elizabeth tirelessly created the photo section of the Life Book and began writing, editing, and re-editing her biography. She wanted it to reflect the best, and God wanted it to reflect her heart.

Elizabeth wouldn't allow herself to think that her heart's desire to hold a child in her arms was even going to be possible until all the paperwork was completed. Twice she allowed herself to do that and then thought, *"No, not until a birth mother picks us."* Elizabeth thought the criterion to complete the application was very intense for the potential adoptive parents but not as much for the birth parents. She and Joe would want to know everything about their child, their birth parents', background, and medical history. Laurie reassured them that by building a personal relationship with the birth parents, they would discover the answers to their questions. Elizabeth wanted something more black and white, more definitive. Still, she remained quiet and accepting of the process, *"this is the way it was done, after all"*.

After submitting the application, months went by and they heard nothing from the agency. Elizabeth tried not to dwell on that fact. She and Joe rarely spoke of it. One day out of the blue Elizabeth couldn't wait any longer and called the agency to ask if any birth mothers had even selected their Life Book. Laurie shared that it had been, a number of times, but possibly the Life Book needed to be jazzed up a bit more. Elizabeth thought, *"Joe and I aren't jazzy people, we poured our heart and soul into the book when creating it. Sharing our thoughts, desires, and ambitions all over the pages"*. Laurie thought perhaps if they looked at other Life Books that would give them some new ideas. Elizabeth felt like a balloon that had just released its air, deflated and small, *"so we weren't good enough"*. She shared that with Joe and his response was to downplay the statement, *"It wouldn't hurt to look at other ideas, would it?"*

Elizabeth just sighed.

Attending monthly support group meetings until picked by a birth mother was one of the requirements the agency enforced. The meetings offered a variety of topics, and attendees ranged from families who had just adopted, families waiting to adopt, and

36

the agencies' staff. The information was valuable and informative and served to increase a better understanding of how the open adoption puzzle was navigated. Listening to stories of how birth mothers and birth fathers interacted with adopted families after the child was born gave Joe and Elizabeth a lot to think about.

During the waiting period, the waiting adoptive parents were asked to volunteer to drive birth mothers to medical appointments and other activities. Those volunteer hours broadened Elizabeth's understanding of birth mothers' feelings and experiences about placing their babies for adoption. At times, hearing their stories broke her heart. Elizabeth slowly realized that her joy of becoming a mother was potentially heartbreaking for her child's birth mother.

She would often pray while driving, *"Lord, be with us all. Help me lead with kindness, love, and grace with every birth mother I interact with. Wrap your loving arms around them. Let them feel your warm and embracing love personally."*

One morning, Elizabeth received a call from the agency and was asked to take one of the girls, Linda, to a doctor's appointment. Quickly, she rearranged her day to accommodate the request. Elizabeth dropped Linda off at the front door, parked the car, and then walked into the doctor's waiting office. As she waited for Linda, Elizabeth's mind was flooded with memories of the two children she had miscarried.

She had been in multiple OB/GYN offices before with other birth mothers. Why were those feelings surfacing today? *"No"*, Elizabeth thought, *"I can't do that now.* "Somehow, someway the desire in her heart to be a Mom would come true, she just knew it. She willed those feelings back down and picked up a magazine. She asked God to just take away the memories, so she could make it through the appointment time and take Linda back home.

Linda was wearing an ankle monitor. Elizabeth didn't notice it at first, but when she got into the car it was quite obvious. It looked awfully uncomfortable; Elizabeth was curious as to why she was wearing it. So, she asked Linda about it. Chuckling a bit, Linda looked at Elizabeth in disbelief as if thinking, *"This woman doesn't even know what an ankle monitor is for? Obviously, she's never been caught."* Linda shared that she was out of jail, and on probation for a drug charge. She was required to wear the ankle monitor during her probationary period. The monitor tracks her location at all times.

Elizabeth took it all in. She had experienced wild days and unwise choices of her own when she was in her late teens and early twenties but had never been caught or arrested. Linda sat in silence for the remainder of the ride home. She was due in four months. In the silence, Elizabeth thought of the life Linda's child would have.

Three weeks later, Elizabeth was contacted to provide another ride for Linda again. It wasn't to a doctor's appointment, but somewhere else. Linda didn't want to disclose the destination; she just wanted an answer. Elizabeth took a breath, *"Lord what should I do? Am I putting myself in danger?"* Linda didn't live in the best part of the city, but she was reaching out. *"Lord, What do you think?"*

Elizabeth was at work, dressed in a suit for an appointment she had earlier in the day, but she could get away and Linda needed help. She told Linda, *"Yes",* and then she asked again where she needed to go. Linda was hesitant to share but finally said, *"I need to go see my parole officer I've had a dirty UDT."* Elizabeth didn't know what a dirty UDT was, or that it was slang for a Urinary Drug Test that displays drug usage, so she asked. Linda laughed out loud, and her response made Elizabeth think, *"She must think I'm really naïve and have never been in precarious situations."* Laughingly Linda answered, *"I had to take a urine test and it showed I had drugs in my system".*

Linda's world was very different from Elizabeth's. She didn't understand it, but she knew God did. Her heart told her it

39

was going to be okay. Off she went to pick up Linda. It took a little bit to find her house. The neighborhood seemed neglected. The houses did not have house numbers, and many were abandoned. Broken-down cars littered the lawns in the much-too-high grass.

Elizabeth's sports car pulled into the driveway, and she waited a minute to get out of the car and walk to the front door. She was dressed for a business meeting and wasn't driving an inconspicuous car, so she was very obvious in the neighborhood. But she felt like the Lord was with her and this was more about helping someone and being obedient to God than anything else. So, she got out of the car, walked up to the front door, and knocked. Linda opened the door and Elizabeth felt a pit in her stomach. The house was filthy, and Elizabeth wanted to pick Linda up and move on.

Linda's girlfriend Shelly was at the house also and Linda told Elizabeth she was going to go with them to the parole office. Oddly, Linda brought a pillowcase filled with clothes, a pillow, and a stuffed animal. They all got back into the car and drove downtown to the parole office. On the drive downtown, Elizabeth asked Linda if she could pray for her. Linda wasn't exactly sure what was going to happen once at her parole officer's office, so she said, *"Sure, I can use all the help I can get."* Elizabeth prayed a simple prayer asking God to protect Linda no matter what happened, to go before her, and give her peace.

Elizabeth's heart was anxious; she hadn't experienced anything like this in a long time. When they walked into the parole officer's waiting room, it was all business; Linda proceeded into her parole officer's inner office immediately. Shelly and Elizabeth sat in the waiting area. Shelly was afraid of what was going to happen to Linda and shared her concerns. She wouldn't stop talking. *"What was Linda going to do? Would she be going back to jail?"*

Elizabeth didn't know the answers and just kept quiet not responding to Shelly. She began to reflect on her past. That could have been so easily her. In her younger years, the choices she had made were not good, which placed her in dangerous and perilous situations. She was glad her life had changed drastically since then in all aspects. Elizabeth felt thankful that God's hedge of protection had been over her even then, and a little sad when she realized that He had been helping her all the time. She hadn't even known He was there.

Linda came out of the parole officer's office with the parole officer right behind her. He offered Linda the opportunity to remove her jewelry and give Shelly her belongings. The officer stated, *"You're coming with me. Remove your jewelry you can't*

41

take it with you where you're going." Linda did as instructed, said a quick goodbye, and she was gone.

Elizabeth sat there, taking this all in, wondering how the baby felt inside Linda's womb. Her heart broke for the baby and Linda. She would deliver her child in prison. Linda was 18 years old, and this was the second time she would do time in jail for drugs. Elizabeth thought, *"Lord take care of her. She's going to have a child and she's just a child herself. Why do things like this happen? Why can't people who so desperately want children have them, and those who don't necessarily want children seem to have them?"*

And God answered.

In her inner being, Elizabeth sensed what she believed to be God's voice, *"Elizabeth, follow me and be obedient".*

When Elizabeth returned to her office after taking Shelly and Linda's things back to Linda's house, she was mentally exhausted as her thoughts pondered all she had experienced. Trying to grasp what Linda's life was like. What were the circumstances surrounding Linda's baby? How did Shelly fit into the picture? How addicted to drugs was Linda? Was the baby addicted to drugs? Where was her mother, her family? Why did

God ask Elizabeth to provide a ride, and walk through the activities of the day?

She decided to leave work early, and once at home, the telephone rang. It was Laurie Jackson, the Executive Director of the adoption agency. Elizabeth couldn't believe it her thoughts went to what she felt God share earlier in the day, *"Elizabeth, follow me and be obedient."*

Excited, Laurie gave Elizabeth the news. A couple had reviewed their Life Book and would like to talk to them. Laurie continued, *"Could the birth mother call that evening?"* Elizabeth slid down into the chair by the phone as her mind raced, *"Did she just hear what she thought she did? A birth mother looked at our Life Book and liked it? It wasn't jazzed up."* Elizabeth hurriedly regained her thoughts and simply answered, *"Yes"*. The details regarding the time and her name were shared and then the call ended. Elizabeth held the phone in her hand and a thought trickled through her mind, *"Is this really going to happen, Lord?"*

Joe came home from work and Elizabeth shared the news. He was pleased. The events of the day had taken a toll on her, and she was tired but very excited. The telephone rang and it was Audrey, the birth mother, the one who picked their unjazzy Life Book. Elizabeth didn't quite know what to say but somehow, together they engaged in a conversation. Audrey shared that she was living with the baby's birth father, Sam. They had used protection and were surprised when she found out she was pregnant. Elizabeth learned that they planned on getting married, but not having children, and they lived in a suburb of the city Joe and Elizabeth lived in. After talking for about an hour, they decided the four of them should meet and set a time for the following week.

The following Tuesday night they met at a Mexican restaurant and the dinner visit proved to be a real challenge. Sam was extremely introverted and withdrawn. The entire situation seemed to be overwhelming to him, conversing with him was extremely limited. It wasn't that he didn't want to talk and contribute; he just didn't know what to say and was so shut down by Audrey. Audrey pretty much steered the ship in their relationship. She tried to control the conversation and Sam, and at times it was too much. Elizabeth felt for Sam and wondered how the next six weeks were going to go if they picked them as their adoptive couple.

Audrey shared that her baby girl was due on June 3rd, and she wanted Elizabeth to start attending her doctor's appointments with her. The doctor knew Audrey was placing the baby for adoption. There were six weeks before the baby was to be born, so this would give Elizabeth plenty of time to get to know the doctor,

Audrey, and the baby much better. She also shared where the baby would be born, what she wanted at the hospital, and how the process was going to proceed.

Audrey's next doctor's appointment was within two weeks, and she wanted Elizabeth to be present. Elizabeth attended, and it proved to be a real eye-opener. Audrey's doctor wasn't open to letting Elizabeth inside the examining room. The doctor shared quite emphatically that she was concerned that Audrey wouldn't feel open to sharing how she was really feeling if Elizabeth were in the room. Their doctor/patient relationship would be compromised, and, in her opinion, there wasn't a need for Elizabeth to be in the room ... period.

Elizabeth felt like a MAC truck had hit her squarely in the face. From what she had heard in the adoption support group meetings, as well as what Audrey had shared at dinner when they met, she wanted Elizabeth to be there, plus this was a time when the birth and adoptive mothers could bond before the baby was born and experience the growth and development of the baby still in the womb. Elizabeth wasn't expecting this reaction. It was obvious either the doctor didn't like the fact that Audrey was placing the baby up for adoption, didn't like Elizabeth, Audrey set Elizabeth up or had a problem herself. Elizabeth's mind raced to take in all this new information and then process it.

Audrey acted really cool and collected when she left the examining room. Like she was feeling pleased she had just trumped Elizabeth. Elizabeth felt like she was set up and inwardly decided that she wasn't going to put herself in that position again. Nothing was said about the incident. Elizabeth now knew she was at Audrey's mercy, and Audrey knew it too. Over the next six weeks, similar situations emerged, and Elizabeth kept herself guarded. She prayed that God would protect Audrey's baby girl and keep her from harm and danger – whatever that might be in the supernatural or natural.

Even though they had decided to adopt, a desire lingered in Elizabeth's heart to breastfeed her children. After losing two children, however, the option didn't feel very real. When Elizabeth and Laurie first talked about adoption, Laurie had asked Elizabeth if she was going to breastfeed, which baffled Elizabeth and she asked, *"How could that happen? I wanted to breastfeed but didn't think it was an option because I'm adopting a child?"* Laurie chuckled and responded, *"It happens all the time."*

Laurie shared excitedly, for adoptive mothers the breastfeeding process begins weeks or months before the baby is born. Advanced planning is required, but once the baby arrives adoptive breastfeeding is possible. Laurie provided information on the La Leche League, an international organization that organizes advocacy, education, and training related to breastfeeding.

Elizabeth contacted the organization and read everything she could about breastfeeding adoptive children. She talked with Joe about the option, and he told her to go for it. A soothing thought touched her heart *"My dream was becoming a reality – Thank you, Jesus."*

With the breast pump rented, Elizabeth charged forward bringing the pump to work and organizing her workday around a schedule, which allowed three fifteen-minute sessions of pumping during the workday. Staying on schedule would likely produce the milk production needed, so that when her daughter was born, Elizabeth would be ready.

At one of their adoption support group meetings, Elizabeth shared the experiences she was having with Audrey and how she had to guard her heart and mind, and at times felt like Audrey was setting traps for her. These experiences were challenging at best, and she wanted to hear other adoptive parents' thoughts regarding them. Thankfully the group empathized with Elizabeth and shared their own experiences relating to their birth mothers. The unexpected and expected, Elizabeth appreciated their support as she realized that these people totally understood her feelings and responses and empathized with her.

Laurie knew how challenging a relationship with Audrey could be. After the meeting, Laurie pulled Elizabeth aside and disclosed her feelings, *"I appreciate the way you are handling your relationship with Audrey and Sam. I can't think of a more mature couple to do so, Thank you."* She understood the challenges in front of them, and as much as Elizabeth appreciated her support, she thought, *"Why does this have to be so difficult? Why does the process cause such heartache? Why does it seem like, I always get the most challenging situations?"*

Elizabeth was ready to experience an event or activity that wasn't as taxing, but as she lingered with that thought, she was reminded that birthing a child, the labor, pushing and post-delivery is an extremely painful process.

--TAKE AWAY--

- Obedience, what does it mean?

1 Corinthians 15:58 "So, my dear brothers and sisters, be strong and immovable. Always work enthusiastically for the Lord, for you know that nothing you do for the Lord is ever useless."

Psalm 128:1 "Blessed are all who fear the Lord who walk in obedience to him."

Mark 12:29-30 "The most important commandment is this: 'Listen, O Israel! The Lord our God is the one and only Lord. And you must love the Lord your God with all your soul, all your mind, and all your strength'. The second is equally important: 'Love your neighbor as yourself.'"

When you love God completely and wholeheartedly and care for others as you care for yourself, you are following God's command. Be a servant, with a servant's heart, step out into unchartered waters, and follow God. Be open and unguarded to the way God wants you to serve. It takes faith, but God never asks you to do things alone. He is always right beside you. Take His hand. He will guide you through any unknown territory. Don't let discouragement over lack of results keep you from doing the work of the Lord obediently.

Chapter 4 - It's Going to Happen

Elizabeth's parents were making their annual return trip from Arizona to New York. Spending the winter in Arizona made her Dad John's heart swell. He loved warm weather and compared to the winter weather in New York, Arizona was paradise. Irene, his wife, didn't hold the same passion for Arizona. Her life was her family and being away from them caused a bit of friction between her and John.

Just before Easter every year they began their trip back to New York and always stopped to see Joe and Elizabeth on the way. This was the one-time Elizabeth got to see her parents. Joe and Elizabeth didn't vacation in New York very often and her parents didn't visit them unless they drove back to New York via the southern route from Arizona.

Elizabeth had shared with them that she and Joe had been chosen by Audrey and Sam to be the adoptive parents of their baby girl. John and Irene felt their excitement and her Dad shared eagerly this would be their seventeenth grandchild.

Always repurposing and fixing things around the house, John was green before green was "cool". When they visited Elizabeth and Joe, he would often fix a multitude of items that needed tending to and Elizabeth looked forward to that. Sometimes he even fixed things they weren't aware needed fixing! Irene and Elizabeth got along well and enjoyed their time together when they visited.

John and Irene were up for a challenge that visit, and they started helping Joe and Elizabeth clean out the garage, nothing like bonding over household chores. The morning ensued with substantial progress until a phone call came. It was Laurie, the Executive Director of the adoption agency. Audrey and Sam were out shopping that morning and Audrey's water broke. They drove straight to the hospital to have Audrey checked and verify she and the baby were fine. Having never had a baby, Elizabeth asked Laurie, *"So what's the next step?* Laurie chuckled and said, *"You and Joe need to come to the hospital - you're going to have a baby"*.

Elizabeth sheepishly hung up the phone, looked at Joe, and said, *"We're going to have a baby today"*. Her Dad hugged her and said, *"Just leave everything. We'll take care of returning things back into the garage."* Elizabeth's thoughts took off in high gear, although it seemed like she and Joe were moving in slow motion. It was really happening – the time was now. Elizabeth pinched herself to check to see if she was dreaming.

They arrived at the hospital and found Audrey and Sam. Audrey was sitting up in bed writing out something regarding her life insurance policy and Sam seemed a bit agitated. Laurie was in the room and welcomed Joe and Elizabeth. The doctor had checked Audrey and verified she was in labor, but Audrey was barely one centimeter dilated. It was going to be a long day and possibly night to make it to ten centimeters. Laurie told Joe that a room at the hospital could be purchased for parents who needed a place to sleep. Joe said that sounded like a great idea and went to take care of it.

Audrey's progress was very slow. After a couple of hours and no change, Laurie suggested that Joe and Elizabeth return home and wait for them to call when Audrey was closer to giving birth.

Back home Elizabeth brought her parents up to date on the progress and proceeded to make dinner humming joyfully through the process. Irene began to quiz her about clothes and baby items for their daughter; she noticed Elizabeth didn't seem to be prepared to bring a baby home. When Irene said those words Elizabeth's heart melted. *"A daughter, my daughter – those words never sounded more beautiful."*

Elizabeth had thought she had another six weeks to get ready for their beautiful baby girl and she had picked up only a couple of things, a diaper bag and changing mat. There were no sheets for the bassinet and nothing for their daughter to wear.

53

Elizabeth had shared with her family and friends she wanted to wait for any baby showers until their baby was home. The bassinet they would use was the one Elizabeth used when she was a baby, and she hadn't gotten it out of the attic yet. Irene asked again during dinner about gowns, diapers, and all things that go along with bringing a baby home. Elizabeth's response was, *"Yes, I'll need to get some"* and Irene said firmly, *"Sounds like we'll be getting them tonight."* They both laughed out loud; the realization of it all was slowly coming into focus and after dinner, they went to Target and bought the essentials needed for the baby's homecoming.

Around 10:00 p.m. Audrey called and shared that she was six centimeters dilated and that Elizabeth and Joe should come to the hospital. Elizabeth found Laurie, Sam, and Audrey in the labor and delivery unit and was allowed into the room, graciously with open arms. Jane, who happened to be a good friend of Laurie's, was Audrey's labor and delivery nurse. With a warm smile and friendly face, she had been through the process of birth and adoptive mothers being in the labor and delivery room together and didn't miss a beat making everyone feel at ease.

Audrey's doctor, who never acknowledged Elizabeth, appeared in the room just in time to deliver the baby. Additional staff from the Pediatric Intensive Care Unit were called in due to Audrey's delivery being six weeks early.

In a crowded room at 3:43 a.m. on March 31st, Catherine Elizabeth was born. She weighed 5 lbs. 11 ½ ounces and cried a sweet cry that filled Elizabeth's heart with joy and excitement. Elizabeth stood by Audrey's bed and tears flowed out of her like Niagara Falls, she continued to thank and praise God for the beautiful experience of seeing their daughter brought into this life.

Audrey's doctor had asked Sam if he wanted to cut the umbilical cord and he said an emphatic, *"No"*. Audrey then asked Elizabeth if she wanted to, and she did. Cutting the cord felt like cutting a thick rubber hose. When you think of what the umbilical cord's function is, it had to be thick and tough to carry the food, oxygen, and waste to and from the placenta. It was like a significant rite of passage for Elizabeth; Catie's adoptive mom cut the physical connection from Audrey, Catie's birth mother. As emotionally painful as it was for Audrey to let go and follow the adoptive plan she had made for Catie, the happiness that Elizabeth felt deep within her heart was bubbling over.

Catie's APGAR score test was completed, and she passed with flying colors so there was no need for extra medical care. After the APGAR test was completed, Audrey wanted to breastfeed Catie and Laurie assisted Audrey in doing so. It took more courage than Elizabeth had originally thought to agree with Audrey's request. Catie wouldn't latch on to Audrey's breast even after numerous attempts and the sadness in Audrey's eyes displayed a deep disappointment.

About that time Elizabeth left to go find Joe and bring him into the labor and delivery room. The sight of blood, and smell of amniotic fluid, etc. would have placed Joe on the floor had he stayed in the delivery room for his daughter's birth, but he was ready to meet his daughter after her delivery.

He proudly held his daughter, searching her face and checking out her ten tiny fingers and toes. She was little but not a preemie as the delivery team originally thought. He thought she was just perfect and fell in love with her immediately.

Finally getting settled into a normal private hospital room, Elizabeth and Catie started the bonding process. Audrey's adoption plan was being implemented as she had requested but it was obvious the plan was harder to accept than she had ever anticipated. The room was large and provided a sitting area with a foldout couch on the opposite side of where Audrey's hospital bed was located.

Elizabeth took Catie into her arms and studied her. Every inch of Catie was beautiful, the most beautiful baby Elizabeth had ever seen – just perfect. Her button nose, pretty face, ten tiny fingers and toes, and her smell and feel were a healing balm to Elizabeth's heart. She fell so deeply in love with Catie that her heart ached.

God knew exactly what Elizabeth desired, and He was faithful. Elizabeth couldn't put her down. A nurse came into the room and shared that it helps newborns to regulate body temperature and soothes them when they experience skin-to-skin contact.

Elizabeth loved the feeling of Catie snuggled on her chest, skin-to-skin as they lay together in the foldout bed. Tears flooded Elizabeth's eyes and heart as she held her daughter. *Thank you, Lord, for giving me the desire of my heart.* Elizabeth felt the Lord saying, *"I've loved you with an everlasting love Elizabeth, I am with you."*

Audrey was staring at Elizabeth and Catie when Laurie entered the hospital room, and she went over to Audrey first. As Elizabeth soaked up the skin-to-skin contact with Catie, she thought, *"This must be so hard for Audrey, my ultimate joy, is her undying pain. Be with her Lord, help me to be kind and loving."* Laurie smiled at Elizabeth and asked if she had breastfed Catie yet. Laurie assisted Elizabeth and Catie latched on to Elizabeth's breast immediately. A smile came across Elizabeth's face, which came from the depths of her heart. Another miracle! *"Thank you, Lord"*.

The week before Catie was born, Elizabeth was showering on a Saturday morning and noticed the water had a cloudy white appearance. She was curious as nothing had flowed from her body like that before, and then she stood really still. It was breast milk. The heat from the hot shower and moist washcloth triggered the breast milk to express. Elizabeth began to weep. God continued to be present and faithful every step in the process of becoming a Mother. *"Oh, how He loves me"*, Elizabeth thought.

The weeks of pumping her breasts in fifteen-minute intervals three times a day at the office had proven beneficial.

Elizabeth didn't want Catie to stop feeding. To hold her so close and experience the physical bonding between them was a desire Elizabeth had in her heart for so long. She was a Mom to a beautiful, wonderful, healthy baby girl, just like she had desired for so many years. Was this a dream? If only her Mom could have been with them and shared that moment.

Later in the day, Elizabeth's parents came up to meet their seventeenth grandchild and so did her friend Elizabeth W. The pleasure of sharing Catie with family and friends was a treasured experience. They each met Audrey and then asked Audrey to join in their time together as family and friends.

Leaving the hospital the following day was hard for both Audrey and Elizabeth. Audrey had asked if she could spend some time alone with Catie prior to leaving. Elizabeth agreed and left the hospital room. Elizabeth couldn't imagine the conversation Audrey had with her. She began searching her heart for the words she would say in Audrey's situation.

Audrey had carried Catie for nine months. She knew her sleep and wake patterns, what type of music she responded to, and what foods bothered her, and Elizabeth felt sure Audrey dreamed about her. Although Audrey always referred to Catie as "Joe and Elizabeth's baby", Elizabeth wondered if she ever thought about changing her mind about placement. Did Audrey want to share with Catie why she chose adoption for her? In her heart, after meeting Catie, holding her, and realizing she was her daughter, could she really place Catie with Joe and Elizabeth to raise as their own?

Even though Audrey had made an open adoption plan for Catie, there were many specifics not outlined after Catie was born. Elizabeth wondered if she pondered those thoughts, as the time seemed to rush by. How gut-wrenchingly painful it must be.

Elizabeth had returned to the hospital room and Sam happened to be right behind her. He asked Elizabeth about moving the discharge process forward. He then approached Audrey and said in a very monotone voice, *"You need to give her up that was the plan."*

Audrey placed Catie in Elizabeth's arms and slowly got out of bed, changed clothes, and walked with Sam to the nurse's station. Something wasn't right. Audrey came back into the room filled with frustration and anger piercing in her eyes and demanded that Elizabeth go to the nurse's station and deal with the issue. Audrey became very distant and cold, and Elizabeth couldn't imagine what had happened or how she was going to resolve it. Elizabeth's thoughts lingered ... *"A representative from the adoption agency would be really helpful right now."* Audrey's discharge paperwork was incorrect, and Elizabeth gave the nurse a pleading look to help facilitate the issue to resolution. The mistake was identified, and Elizabeth asked Audrey and Sam to join her at the nurse's station. Signatures were obtained and the discharge paperwork was completed. Audrey and Sam walked to the elevator in silence.

Elizabeth didn't know what to do, she had Catie in her arms and it was obvious that Audrey wanted nothing to do with either of them. She had a scowl on her face that shouted, *"Leave me alone, I don't want to leave but I have to. You have Catie now; go away."* The moment was very awkward. As the elevator door closed, Elizabeth held Catie very tightly and went to find Joe.

As Elizabeth reflected on what had just transpired, she thought about her relationship with Audrey over the last six weeks. Always on guard, feeling like the next step was a trap, yet at times it seemed that Audrey wanted Elizabeth to be her own mother and Elizabeth tried to support her as best she could. Encouraging her, taking her to lunch, shopping, driving her to the weekly doctor appointments, and waiting in the waiting room instead of joining Audrey. Elizabeth felt like Audrey was trying to control her and play head games with her, causing Elizabeth to always be on guard not aware of Audrey's next move. Their relationship never seemed to flow and that saddened Elizabeth. Members of their adoption support group had better relationships with their birth mothers. Elizabeth couldn't figure out what was wrong, but she did know that she wasn't going to allow Audrey to manipulate her.

She thought of what Laurie had shared with her, *"I'm glad you and Joe are Audrey and Sam's adoptive parents. Your grace and maturity go before you when interacting with them".* Laurie had gotten to know Sam and Audrey during the pregnancy and realized that having a relationship with either of them at this time wasn't going to be easy.

These thoughts didn't make Elizabeth feel all that comforted, the interactions with Audrey prior to Catie's birth really stretched her emotionally. At one point, Elizabeth contacted Laurie regarding Audrey's response and reaction to the regular doctor visits and other issues that arose. Laurie was as perplexed as Elizabeth and shared, *"The only thing I can share is one of my favorite verses in Isaiah 43:2. When you go through deep waters, I will be with you. When you go through rivers of difficulty you will not drown. When you walk through the fire of oppression you will not be burned up; the flames will not consume you."* Elizabeth often looked to the Bible for comfort and wisdom and felt blessed when she found a scripture and encouragement to handle her concerns. She appreciated Laurie sharing the verses. The only action Elizabeth knew to do was pray. So that's what she did, she personalized those verses and hung onto the promises.

Laurie met Joe and Elizabeth at the hospital to discharge Catie, per adoption agency protocol, and walked her out to the waiting car. The sun was shining brightly just like Joe and Elizabeth's heart. They were thrilled to be a family and couldn't wait to get home.

Irene had washed all of Catie's clothes. John got the bassinet out of the attic and set it up and washed it awaiting her arrival. Catie snuggled in her new bed like it was made just for her.

The bassinet that Elizabeth used as a baby now held her precious daughter. As Elizabeth placed Catie into the bassinet those precious ties to Elizabeth's Mom flooded her heart.

Thankfully, Elizabeth's parents extended their stay an extra week to help and support them with all the new activities and lack of sleep Elizabeth and Joe experienced. A new baby brought drastic schedule changes, but Elizabeth absolutely loved every moment of every day. Catie was an easy baby. The breast-feeding was working very well, and a rhythm was slowly beginning to come together.

Audrey came over to see Catie often, whenever she could. It almost became too much and one night Elizabeth called Laurie and asked for advice. Because there wasn't a schedule in place, Audrey seemed to show up at any time, and sometimes it wasn't at the best times. It was becoming apparent that a schedule needed to be implemented. Elizabeth wasn't looking forward to having that conversation with Audrey. The more Audrey was at their house, the more it felt like Audrey wanted to co-parent and cross boundaries and push as much as she could. Knowing how to delicately handle her strong personality and odd way of handling issues wasn't something Elizabeth looked forward to or knew how to handle.

Laurie agreed that a schedule would be a good idea. She suggested including options, and defining boundaries, and encouraged Elizabeth to meet with Audrey right away. Never having been in a similar situation, Elizabeth wished Laurie had given more advice and direction, or at least offered to meet with them.

Elizabeth invited Audrey to lunch. She thought having the conversation at a restaurant might be easier. Being on neutral ground with the distraction of lunch and other people. Audrey was friendly and seemed to have looked forward to seeing Catie. As the conversation started, Audrey asked to hold Catie. She was snug on Elizabeth's chest in a baby sling, not sleeping but content. Elizabeth placed her into Audrey's arms and Audrey held her close, smelling her sweet baby girl, and looked longingly into Catie's face and eyes. Elizabeth slowly realized the conversation was going to be even more of a challenge than she had anticipated.

She didn't want to isolate Catie from Audrey at all. She was just going to ask for a plan and a schedule to be followed, rather than an open-door policy of Audrey dropping by anytime. Mixed feelings emerged in Elizabeth's heart as she tried to begin speaking. She couldn't fathom Audrey's feelings. The pain of placing a baby with another family was too much to imagine.

As Elizabeth began the conversation and shared why she asked Audrey to lunch. Audrey's response was very direct, loaded, and stung Elizabeth's heart. But now the topic was out on the table. A schedule would be the best way to handle visits, communication, and contact. Audrey roared back, *"Will I ever see her again? This is why I chose open adoption so I could see my child when I wanted to. Not when you want me to see her."*

Sharing that she and Joe were not asking for her to stay away but to follow a schedule that would work best for everyone wasn't received well, no matter what Elizabeth said, Audrey wasn't hearing it. She clung to Catie, and her body became rigid. Her cold piercing eyes communicated louder than her words. After a long bit of silence, Audrey thrust Catie into Elizabeth's arms and said, *"Here take her. She's yours."*

Elizabeth acted in slow motion as her head and heart were processing what she had just experienced. What she had thought was going to be a challenging conversation, seemed to have turned into a one-sided war. Elizabeth paid the bill in silence and then excused herself from the table. She and Catie left. Once she reached the car, she broke down and cried. Hard. This was too much. God, we are both hurting.

Elizabeth cried out to God," *Help me, I didn't mean to hurt or devastate Audrey I've tried to be kind, loving, and available throughout the entire process. Where do I go from here?"*

And Elizabeth was gently reminded by God .....

"When you go through deep waters, I will be with you. When you go through rivers of difficulty you will not drown. When you walk through the fire of oppression you will not be burned up; the flames will not consume you"

Weeks ensued before Elizabeth heard anything from Audrey. Audrey finally called and asked if she could come over and see Catie. The time together wasn't uncomfortable and Audrey enjoyed seeing Catie and had fun.

In Elizabeth's heart, she felt the separation may have given Audrey time to think the situation through and become at peace with it, at least she wanted to believe that. Elizabeth and Audrey never talked about it again. They saw each other occasionally and respected each other's boundaries.

--TAKE AWAY--

- Stand in Faith.

Luke 6:27-28 "But to you who are willing to listen, I say, love your enemies. Do good to those who hate you. Bless those who curse you. Pray for those who hurt you."

Isaiah 43:1-2 "Do not be afraid, for I have ransomed you. I have called you by name; you are mine. When you go through deep waters I will be with you. When you go through rivers of difficulty, you will not drown. When you walk through the fire of oppression, you will not be burned up; the flames will not consume."

Practicing God's word every day will help you stand in faith. Build your life on the bedrock of Jesus and His message regardless of what is happening in your life. Use God's word as a sword to remove the evil one's thoughts and snares. Handle the battles thrown your way with the word of God. He will always stand by your side and His provisions are the best. When you feel there are no words left, pray the word of God. Going through rivers of difficulty can cause you to grow stronger. If you go in your own strength, you are more likely to drown. If you invite the Lord to go with you, He will protect you.

A DREAM COME TRUE

PART III: OBEDIENCE

Chapter 5 - A Real Surprise

"Who would have thought? What a shock?" The words tumbled out of Elizabeth's mouth, words that never would have been said four years ago.

Raising Catie brought such joy to Elizabeth and Joe's hearts. Walking together strolling Catie in her stroller in their neighborhood. Watching her climb up the slide on her own and then hearing her shout with joy when she slid down. Seeing the smile on her face and her hands reaching up toward them when she awoke in the morning, each milestone brought sheer delight to Joe and Elizabeth.

Their life was complete and full, although drastically different than what had been their pre-Catie normal. Elizabeth loved being a Mom. It filled her days to capacity with all things Catie. Teaching, sharing, and loving reminded Elizabeth of her own Mom, and being able to do those things with Catie filled Elizabeth's heart.

So, she didn't notice when she was late and didn't think a thing about it. With all of the infertility issues Joe and Elizabeth experienced, Elizabeth just dismissed it. That had happened many times before.

When she was late the following month, Elizabeth thought perhaps she should check things out. On a diaper run to the drug store, Elizabeth picked up a pregnancy test. She didn't feel pregnant, but she thought she'd take a chance and see if she was. She couldn't be pregnant, but thought, why not check and see?

Once home, after she put things away, she watched Catie cruising in the living room and pulling up on the couch, then rocking back and forth, then dropping to the floor and start crawling again. As Elizabeth watched her, she thought, *"If I am pregnant, wow these children will be close in age! Hope I have the stamina to keep up."* She dismissed the thought and began fixing dinner and prepared for Joe to come home from work.

After dinner and time with her Daddy, it was time for Catie to bathe and then go to bed. After Elizabeth tucked Catie into bed, she realized she hadn't taken the pregnancy test, and then chuckled to herself. Whenever she had taken a pregnancy test before it was with great anticipation and desire. It was her only focus. She would have never forgotten to do it.

After straightening up the house and throwing a load of laundry in the washer, Elizabeth realized how tired she was and began getting ready to go to bed. As she brushed her teeth, she waited for the pregnancy test to show its results. She hadn't said anything to Joe yet, but she knew he would be very surprised if indeed she was pregnant. Who was she kidding Elizabeth herself would be surprised!

Standing in the bathroom, the little red line showed brightly. Elizabeth just stared at it in disbelief. Who would have thought after all she and Joe went through to start a family? The losses and heartache, the tests, the words that people meant for encouragement, which felt so empty and sterile. Elizabeth didn't know how to feel.

After Catie was born Elizabeth didn't think about getting pregnant and pushed all the infertility issues from her heart and mind. There wasn't any need to use protection and so Elizabeth and Joe didn't. Their life was very fulfilled and Catie completed their family.

Thinking about being pregnant stirred up the painful memories Elizabeth had during their path to parenthood. Failed procedures, two miscarriages, and exhaustion from all aspects of treatment, injectable medications, the monthly anticipation, and resulting disappointment with failed pregnancy tests were just too much. Flashbacks of those experiences were brought to the forefront of Elizabeth's mind and her emotions went wild. Would this baby she was carrying be another statistic in her life?

"Lord, help me process all of these feelings", Elizabeth prayed, *"If this is the next step in our journey, allow this child inside of me to grow. Become the healthy brother or sister you have for Catie."* It was times like these that Elizabeth missed her own Mother so much.

Seeking out other women and couples that were struggling with infertility and talking about their experiences wasn't something Joe and Elizabeth did. Spending time with friends that had new babies and young children wasn't easy. It seemed everywhere Elizabeth looked there was another pregnant woman, a baby shower invitation, or a christening/dedication event to attend. That time in their life was hard. Elizabeth felt alone, overwhelmed, and a failure. Joe never made her feel that way she brought it on herself.

As Elizabeth pondered over the last years of their life, the sense of powerlessness that infertility brought was very real. Each month Elizabeth and Joe completed another treatment cycle, they hoped for the best, but they knew they had little or no control over the outcome. Past Mother's Day memories were hard. Not only because Elizabeth thought of her own Mother and how she was taken too early in her life, but the fact that she couldn't get

72

pregnant no matter what she and Joe tried. The pain and grief washed over her all over again.

Joe came into the bedroom and Elizabeth shared the news. He was as surprised as she was. When Elizabeth shared her thoughts about this baby just being another statistic in their life, Joe tenderly said, *"Let's not go there,* Elizabeth. *We'll take this one step at a time."*

Elizabeth didn't know how to react to Joe's response and struggled to go to sleep. The thoughts of their journey to parenthood continually cycled through her mind. *"Oh Jesus, help me to leave all of this in your hands"*, she prayed. *"It's way too big for me to handle I can't do this alone again,"* and as she prayed, she felt God pouring into her heart. *"When you go through deep waters and great trouble, I will be with you. When you go through rivers of difficulty, you will not drown. When you walk through the fire of oppression, you will not burn up, the flames will not consume you."* Elizabeth's heart felt such love that only her heavenly Father could give. She knew He would walk right beside her and strengthen her just like he had before.

The following morning was busy, and Elizabeth wanted to cross off her list as many things as she could. A thought that continued to pop into her mind while running errands was to call the doctor. Elizabeth dismissed it. She couldn't be that far along and she was tired and just wanted to get home.

She laid down and took a nap when Catie did and felt better after they woke up. Upon waking, the thought of calling the doctor continued to repeat itself and Elizabeth finally went ahead and called to make an appointment.

Being a regular patient had its benefits, and as Elizabeth was talking with the office to obtain the appointment, she brought them up to date on how Catie was doing. She could be seen in three weeks. Elizabeth just wanted to put this behind her and stop all the concern that was welling up inside of her. She and baby were going to be fine.

Joe was pleased that Elizabeth had made the appointment. From his perspective, there wasn't a need to be excited or concerned, just cautious in relation to Elizabeth and the baby's health. Being calm and handling situations realistically was Joe's approach. Joe wasn't one to let things bother him outwardly and didn't want anyone else overly concerned until it was necessary.

Elizabeth was still providing accounting support to Joe's consulting firm at home. She usually worked when Catie napped. If she worked a little each day, it was much easier to stay current. Often Catie and Elizabeth both went up to the office and Joe enjoyed the distraction, plus it provided an outlet and connection to the firm for Elizabeth.

Trying not to think about the child growing inside her womb, the day finally came, and she was once again in her doctor's office completing another set of labs and an ultrasound. She knew the process very well. Elizabeth knew if she asked the technician to share what they were seeing on the monitor they wouldn't tell her, it was protocol after all. So, she waited for the doctor and didn't even bother to ask them.

When the doctor came in, he welcomed Elizabeth warmly and jumped right to the point. Elizabeth appreciated that about him. He wasn't one to hold back and always gave her the news head-on. Even in a tough situation, he was kind, direct, and factual. "Elizabeth, *I don't have good news the fetus is not growing, and I believe we need to complete a D&C.*" There it was – out on the table, another statistic for Elizabeth and Joe. Elizabeth didn't really react. She was just numb. The emotion welling up inside was familiar. The roller coaster ride she experienced before became a reality once again. Her womb would never be blessed with a child and the emotional force almost took her under.

The surgery would allow the doctor to see the current condition of Elizabeth's uterus and verify if there were any new cysts or tumor growth. The doctor didn't want to prolong the surgery, and the date was set for the following week. Preparations were made regarding childcare for Catie, the house was cleaned, and the accounting was current. Elizabeth was ready to move forward and put all of this behind her. It brought up so many memories. Elizabeth's Mother-in-law, Betty, graciously came and spent the day with Catie, and Joe took Elizabeth to the hospital. The procedure was outpatient, so Joe stayed the day with Elizabeth.

Once the procedure was completed, Elizabeth returned to her outpatient room, and she struggled with pain. Later in the day, her bed sheets were spotted with blood, which wasn't expected. The surgeon had found numerous fibroid tumors which cause abnormal bleeding, and it was determined that Elizabeth needed to be observed for more than twenty-three hours.

Elizabeth's outpatient stay turned into an inpatient hospital stay and she appreciated the fact that she didn't have to leave. She was weak and very tired.

In the evening Betty came to see her, she was concerned and just held Elizabeth's hand sharing what a wonderful day she and Catie had together. Betty's sharing was exactly what Elizabeth needed to hear. Sweet, adorable, Catie, the child that made Elizabeth's heart swell with joy, the child that made Elizabeth a

Mom. She loved her so much and couldn't wait to get home and hold her in her arms.

When Elizabeth returned home, Betty offered to stay the week to help. Since Elizabeth couldn't lift Catie that was confusing to her, so she just got down on the floor and played, read, laughed, and loved her. Betty was so easy to be around, and Elizabeth enjoyed her very much. She graciously cared for all of them and kept the household running. Catie loved having her Grammy at her house and Betty loved being with Catie.

The recovery process proved to be a challenge and Elizabeth wasn't improving as quickly as she hoped. Six months had gone by, and her cycles were worse than ever before and the loss of blood during them was becoming an issue. She would be off her feet for up to ten days and that wasn't easy taking care of a small child.

Back to the doctor for answers and a plan of action, Elizabeth didn't know what to expect but knew something needed to change. The doctor was surprised to see her when he walked into the room and asked. *"Elizabeth why are you here today?"* He read her chart, and Elizabeth shared what she'd been experiencing. Intense cramps, pain that was more than normal, passing blood clots, and the amount of time her cycle lasted could be up to ten days, which was abnormal for her. Plus, she was in bed most of those ten days.

The doctor shared that they found numerous fibroid tumors in her uterus, which were very large. With the pain, blood loss, and other symptoms Elizabeth was experiencing, he didn't want them to burst. His advice was for Elizabeth to have a hysterectomy, *"Let's just take the rest of your reproductive system out. You have only one remaining ovary and with your medical history I don't want to wait"*.

As Elizabeth listened to what the doctor was saying, she couldn't get her head around it. What he was suggesting was too much for Elizabeth to process. Her road to motherhood was eventful, filled with loss and success. God brought Catie into Elizabeth and Joe's life and made them parents. But having a hysterectomy was the end of the road for Elizabeth's womb. In her heart had she really given up hope on ever having a child of Joe's?

Elizabeth drove home very slowly and weary. She was happy to see Catie and held her in her arms for a long time. Elizabeth was so thankful that Catie could always make her heart happy. Catie brought Elizabeth one of her favorite Veggie Tale movies and before Elizabeth placed it into the VCR, they began singing one of Catie's favorite songs from the movie.

"Peter and John Went to Pray"

Peter and John went to pray

They met a lame man on the way

He asked for alms and held out his palms

And this is what Peter did say.

Silver and Gold have I none

But such as I have, give I thee

In the name of Jesus Christ

Of Nazareth rise up and walk

He went walking and leaping and Praising God

Walking and leaping and Praising God

In the name of Jesus Christ of Nazareth rise up and walk.

As they sang together, Elizabeth would always act out the song and Catie would try to mimic her. Often, they would end up laughing and singing together, especially when Elizabeth started walking and leaping. Elizabeth reflected on the lyrics of the song. They were very applicable to her situation. She needed to rise up, walk, and praise God for all that He is and had done in her life. Elizabeth thanked God for using Catie in this situation to help pull her out of despair and turn it around for good. Elizabeth thought,

"Catie was growing up quick, too quick, it was hard to believe she was already eighteen months old."

Surprisingly, Joe came home with dinner and Elizabeth was thrilled! Catie wanted to watch the Veggie Tale movie again, so the three of them enjoyed watching it while eating their dinner. Elizabeth hadn't called Joe after returning from the doctor. She wanted to talk to him face-to-face and share the news. Elizabeth wanted to focus on something else and was so thankful they could eat together and watch a movie even if it was Veggie Tales.

After Elizabeth put Catie to bed, she fell into Joe's arms and shared the doctor's recommendation. It was hard to even say it, hysterectomy, and the reality of a long, desperate battle. Tears filled her broken heart and Elizabeth sobbed, Joe held her and rubbed her back. He didn't know what to say but he knew Elizabeth was strong and had experienced a tremendous amount of pain every month. He wanted the best for her and longed for her pain to end. He knew she needed him to support her as best as he could.

They talked about their journey to parenthood and all they had experienced together, the losses, physical anguish, and up-and-down emotional roller coaster. The excitement of adopting Catie and how instrumental God was in filling their desire. Joe assured Elizabeth that they were in God's hands and His evidence was always proof. Elizabeth listened and knew she had to make a decision, but she wasn't quite ready to do so. Joe respected that and they retired for the night.

Six months later, Elizabeth knew it was time to let go and let God control the situation, and schedule the surgery. God was in the driver's seat and no matter what; He would take care of them like He always did.

Betty and LeRoy willingly accepted the role of caretaker for Elizabeth and Catie during the six weeks after the surgery in their home. Joe worked at the office during the week and spent the weekends with them. His heart was blessed knowing his parents were taking care of his girls.

Thankfully Elizabeth was first on the surgery schedule on the day of her hysterectomy. She needed to be at the hospital at 5:30 a.m. Joe accompanied her to the hospital and Elizabeth was admitted and prepped for surgery. This process was beginning to feel second nature to them. They held hands and prayed while waiting for Elizabeth to be taken to surgery.

As the pre-operative procedures began, Elizabeth didn't feel very strong, she was sick to her stomach and when her blood pressure was taken the nursing staff became alarmed. The stress of knowing what would be happening was on her mind. All Elizabeth knew was she wanted to get on the other side of the surgery. She fainted and things got a bit crazy. Excitement ensued and Elizabeth didn't remember much except the fact that bells and whistles were going off and then it went dark. That's all she remembered until she awoke in her patient room.

The surgery was a success and Joe was glad to see Elizabeth back in her room. The doctor reassured Joe that although there was quite a bit of work to be done, it was completed, and everything looked good. Elizabeth was in and out all afternoon and by dinnertime, she could at least hold a conversation but not a long one. She needed to stay a couple of days and then it was off to her in-laws to recuperate. As Elizabeth lay in her hospital bed, she longed to see Catie. Elizabeth had packed a small picture of her that was on the table beside her bed. That sweet cherub brought joy and laughter to Elizabeth's heart. Betty called to check on Elizabeth and assured her Catie was doing well and waiting for her to come to Grammy's house.

Being alone in the hospital brought back memories that Elizabeth didn't want to relive. Infertility is hard to process. Miscarriages *"Why was it, Lord? Many women can't have children and then there are women that get pregnant that don't want to have children."* Elizabeth thought of Audrey, Catie's birth mother. And then she prayed that God would still her heart and pour His healing balm over the hurt and pain -- release the desire to have a child from her womb because it wasn't going to happen.

The six weeks at Betty and LeRoy's were peaceful and enjoyable. They lived on five acres of land in the country. The grounds were beautiful, and Betty's love for plants and flowers was evident everywhere one looked. The small creek behind the house wasn't always babbling but when it did it was music to one's ears. The birds visited regularly, and Betty enjoyed tending to them providing food and water daily. She knew the type and time of year each bird would come. Cardinals were one of her favorites, the rich red color of their breasts shown beautifully against the lush landscape of her backyard.

LeRoy loved gardening as well. He and his vegetable garden were known in the community where they lived. Weekly, in season, he sold his produce at the Farmer's Market. His family also enjoyed eating the rich rewards during harvest season. Their grandchildren often asked if the vegetables they were enjoying were "Granddaddy's".

Elizabeth received such tender love and care from both LeRoy and Betty. Catie loved being with her grandparents. LeRoy would get down on the floor and play dolls or whatever Catie wanted to do. He would often take Catie to the garden or give her a ride in the wheel barrel. Hearing Catie squeal with delight brought joy to Elizabeth's heart, watching their relationship blossom was a gift that came from God. The kindness LeRoy showed was very endearing. Betty and LeRoy took great care of their daughter-in-law and grandchild. Joe came to visit whenever he could. He missed them both dearly.

One weekend when Joe was visiting and the whole family was watching a movie together, Elizabeth and Joe looked at each other knowing how blessed they were and Joe asked, *"Can we just move in?"* They all laughed simultaneously.

As Elizabeth continued to heal and become stronger, she, Betty, and Catie ventured out to do life's daily routines together. The time to return home was drawing near and Elizabeth and Catie were ready. Joe welcomed them with loving arms on the day of their homecoming.

Home together again as a family, in one piece, ready to take on the next adventure. There was more truth to that statement than they realized.

--TAKE AWAY--

- Letting go of control is not easy, but YOU can do it.

Hebrews 13:5 "Never will I leave you; never will I forsake you."

Jeremiah 10:23-24 "I know, Lord, that our lives are not our own. We are not able to plan our own course. So correct me, Lord, but please be gentle. Do not correct me in anger, for I would die."

Matthew 11:28 "Come to me, all you who are weary and burdened, and I will give you rest."

Philippians 4:8 "And now, dear brothers and sisters, one final thing. Fix your thoughts on what is true, and honorable, and right, and pure, and lovely, and admirable. Think about things that are excellent and worthy of praise."

Letting go of control and releasing the grip is hard to do, but when you follow God and walk obediently it can be done. God will equip you if you begin by first identifying what you can and can't control. Acknowledging that you have an issue is the first step. Surrender to God what you can't control. Freedom begins when we take that first step of surrender. Meditate on the promises that God has given us as His children. Choose a verse that speaks to you. When you feel out of control, say the verse out loud. Say it again until you feel steady. Rest in Jesus. Trust that He is working on your behalf. Be resolved not to act on fear but on Faith through Jesus Christ. Focus your mind and heart on trusting God TODAY!

Chapter 6 - So That's the Reason We Have Two?

With his kidneys working at a 25% capacity, Mike, Elizabeth's brother, didn't know what the next chapter of his life would look like. Up to this point, he had managed his health challenges with only his immediate family knowing what was going on. But now, what options did he have? Would he see his daughters graduate from high school? Would he have the privilege of walking them down the aisle someday? The future wasn't looking very bright. He was in the last inning of the game, and no one was coming to the plate to bat.

Thoughts went to his sister, Elizabeth. She had known all along how bad the situation was. In fact, she was the only family member who knew how sick Mike was. Elizabeth had always told Mike that if he needed a kidney to survive she would give him one of hers she had two!

The drug trial Mike was a part of bought time, but it wasn't working any longer. The kidney disease was progressing, and Mike's health was deteriorating. It was apparent he had to make a choice -- a kidney transplant or dialysis for the rest of his life. As Mike reflected on his choices, he couldn't accept the kidney Elizabeth had always offered to him. She was married now, and her daughter Catie was only two and a half.

It was Mike's choice not to tell anyone in the family about his kidney disease and Elizabeth understood. Their relationship had always been close. When their Mother died, Susie, his girlfriend at the time and now his wife, was visiting the family and was a lifesaver for Elizabeth. Susie had just picked up the pieces and kept the household running so Elizabeth didn't have to. Elizabeth could just exist and grieve. She was fifteen years old and heartbroken, her Mom was her best friend and she was gone.

Elizabeth struggled with all of this. It was too much to process for a teenager. Elizabeth and Mike's Dad were so grief-stricken that he never realized what an effect that losing their Mother would have on his six children. It was tough. Susie was staying with Elizabeth in her room, and she would often try to make her laugh, as her wit and humor were always right on the tip of her tongue.

Preparing meals for the five family members living at home, keeping the house clean, laundry, etc. at just fifteen, was overwhelming. Elizabeth was in high school, and her life was unbearable. She wanted to wake up somewhere else, instead of facing the facts of how her life had changed so drastically, losing her best friend, confidant, and Mom. Abandoned emotionally from her Dad, Elizabeth had nowhere to turn. When Susie went back to

Chicago and she was left alone with all the empty places in her heart, Elizabeth's heart was not only broken but also burdened.

Elizabeth's relationship with Mike and Susie became even closer after that. Once they married, Elizabeth visited them in Chicago often. Her Dad would let her travel to see them for a weekend or in the summer, as it was a quick flight from New York.

As Elizabeth pondered how to pray and help Mike, she thanked God for her family and the precious gift of Catie. If she gave her kidney to Mike would everything work out? In the late summer of that year, Mike began to experience more complications with his kidneys shutting down. He shared with Elizabeth the statistics of the drug trial and basically his options were dialysis, kidney transplant, or die. Always direct and to the point, Mike just stated the facts. Elizabeth also didn't let the grass grow under her feet and started asking Mike about kidney transplantation, possible donors, and life in the future. Her approach was, let's get in front of this instead of following behind it. His daughters were in high school, and Elizabeth knew he wanted to see them grow up and have a fulfilled life. At the rate the disease was deteriorating his kidneys, he was barely going to see them through the end of the year!

Offering to research kidney transplantation from both the donor and recipient's perspective, Elizabeth worked tirelessly and was glad Mike was open to the idea. Pouring over the research, Elizabeth was intently focused. Her home office became 'transplant central'. In two weeks, she had talked with three kidney recipients and two donors. She also found out a transplant surgeon was in her church community group and made an appointment to go see him.

When Mike was first diagnosed with kidney disease, Elizabeth shared that she would give him her kidney. She had two kidneys and their brother David had lived with only one kidney since he was six weeks old it was possible. David had a son born with only one kidney as well and he'd lived a full life. Anything with God was possible, and if all went well, Mike could have the kidney transplant by the end of the year or early the following year.

Mike couldn't accept Elizabeth's gift to donate and would say to her, *"You know you're no poster child for this donation."* But Elizabeth knew in her heart that God had given her this desire and if God wanted her kidney in Mike's body, it didn't matter what her general health was God was going to take care of her. Mike's response saddened Elizabeth and she searched for answers in the Bible. A passage in Hebrews brought comfort and assurance.

"Their weakness was turned to strength. They became strong in battle and put whole armies to flight." Elizabeth just kept praying and believing that God would change Mike's heart.

Elizabeth felt so strongly that she was to donate her kidney. Mike was concerned on a number of fronts. Elizabeth had Catie who was only two years old, what would happen to her if something went wrong, or if Elizabeth would ever have kidney disease what options did she have? Mike struggled with his internal thoughts and concerns about the entire situation and wasn't sure what to do.

Pouring her heart out to God, Elizabeth prayed, *"Lord, the plan is evident, help Mike accept it."* Elizabeth knew God heard prayers ... every single one. As she continued to research and obtain more information on kidney transplants, her routine formed a pattern that consisted of prayer, thanksgiving, research, and printing. Discovering articles that defined a host of issues regarding transplantation, effective treatments, and information about donation flooded her computer. Most everything Elizabeth found, she sent to Mike praying and asking the Holy Spirit to touch his heart and open it to not only receive the new research but also for Mike's spirit to be stirred. Elizabeth's heart's desire was for Mike to understand what type of gift God was giving, not only a physical one but also an opportunity for her brother to accept Christ as his Savior and change his life for eternity.

Conversations regarding other donors within the family were beginning to surface. Jack, their oldest brother who lived in Japan offered to be tested and so did their second brother, Ken as did Susie, Mike's wife.

As Thanksgiving was nearing, Elizabeth felt the need to visit Mike and Susie. So much was coming together and yet things still seemed so unattainable. The need was a feeling from God that Elizabeth had felt before and she knew she needed to act on it.

Elizabeth moved forward in her plan to visit Mike and Susie and made her airline reservations. Once in Chicago, Susie began to share just how bad things really were. Life was rough emotionally and physically for Mike. When he returned home from work, Elizabeth caught a glimpse of him and ducked into another room where she couldn't be seen to gather herself. She was totally taken aback. Mike looked grey, feeble, and exhausted. It took Elizabeth a minute to gather her composure before returning to the kitchen to speak to him. It was all she could do not to burst into tears. She had known things were bad, but actually seeing him, was a hard blow of reality to her emotions.

Prior to leaving for Chicago, Elizabeth had been praying that the donor would be identified by the end of November and Mike would accept what God had for him.

Mike had set up an appointment on Tuesday during the week of Thanksgiving to meet with his kidney transplant coordinator, Doug, at Northwestern Medical Center. Elizabeth happily went with him. She wanted to talk to Doug. She felt in her heart that everything was going to be just fine. Her optimism was contagious and a welcome option for Mike and Susie.

Neither Mike nor Elizabeth was sure how long the appointment would be or if they would get their questions answered. Doug was very receptive and knowledgeable, a helpful straightforward guy. Elizabeth liked him.

After a warm reception, Mike and Elizabeth went to Doug's office and began discussing what was involved in the process and answering Elizabeth's questions. Then without any notice, Doug got up and said, *"Well, let's draw blood and see if* Elizabeth *can be a donor for you"*. He then asked Elizabeth, *"Are you pregnant? How old are you?* At first, Elizabeth was surprised, as the conversation took a very quick turn, and then answered, *"No, I've had a hysterectomy, I'm 41."*

The next thing Elizabeth knew she was feeling a bit faint and there were five tubes of her blood being whisked away to the lab. Doug shared that he was going to Hawaii for the Thanksgiving holiday and wouldn't be returning until the following week. The results of the lab work would be known by then.

Elizabeth's thoughts immediately went to her prayer of asking God for the donor to be identified by the end of November. She stood still in faith, believing they'd have an answer. Doug asked if they would like to see a video of a kidney transplant used for training and Elizabeth quickly said, *"Yes"*. Elizabeth loved watching medical shows and tried to understand terms, procedures, and techniques. With enthusiasm, she and Mike followed Doug into a conference room and began watching the harvesting of a donor's kidney and the process of sewing the kidney into the recipient.

A doctor happened to be walking by the conference room and Doug motioned for him to come in. The doctor just so happened to be the lead kidney specialist on the kidney transplant team at Northwestern. He listened to Doug share Mike's case, and the fact that Elizabeth was being tested as a donor. The doctor's response was, *"Sounds like we have all the participants for a successful surgery"*. At first, Elizabeth felt like Doug and the doctor were kidding around, trying to keep the conversation light. But as the conversation continued, it was obvious that they were serious. The more they talked the more excited Elizabeth got, things were starting to move. Finally, she thought!

If the donor results came back this week, and Elizabeth was identified as a donor and completed the remaining tests, Mike could have his kidney transplant by the end of the year! Even though there were a number of tests to be completed and hoops to be jumped through, it could happen in less than six weeks, especially with God in control.

When Mike and Elizabeth left the meeting, they were both on a high. So much discussed, so much to do, and in only six weeks. On the car ride home, Mike shared how very glad he was that Elizabeth was "steering the ship of the transplant". His physical condition was exhausting him, and he just didn't have the energy to do much of anything else but go to work. Elizabeth warmly accepted the challenge and stayed the course.

Thanksgiving came and Susie made a turkey dinner with all the trimmings. It was delicious! The meal prayer was short and to the point, as Elizabeth prayed, *"Dear God, bless this food, our time together, and for your answers. Amen."*

Friday morning came, and Mike, Susie, and Elizabeth reminisced about the meeting plus other events they'd experienced together in their lives.

In her teens, Elizabeth would often visit Chicago where Mike and Susie lived and "practice" living in a bigger City. One time Elizabeth went to visit Susie's Mother in another part of the city and got lost on the elevated train system, Mike said he had grown grey hair and aged drastically that day. Casually walking into the apartment afterward, not making a big thing about it, Elizabeth was glad she finally made it home. She felt it best not to share what really happened that afternoon. Mike and Susie weren't so casual about it. They had been thinking the worst and told Elizabeth so. For the next fifteen minutes, hot under the collar, and sharing from their hearts the message came across loud and clear. They thought they'd never see Elizabeth again. She was sixteen years old and not familiar with the municipal train system in a major metropolitan city. Laughter ensued as the stories were retold. Now they could laugh about what hadn't been so funny in the first place!

Later in the day, Elizabeth called Northwestern Medical Center to follow up on a number of questions. Mike wanted an idea of what his out-of-pocket expenses for the surgery would be. Joe wanted to know how the transplant team would determine if Elizabeth had two strong working kidneys.

The insurance coverage was verified, and all of the donor testing and surgery would be paid. Mike's portion of the hospital costs would only be 10%, 90% would be covered.

Elizabeth was then transferred to the transplant coordinator's office. The receptionist answered the phone and Elizabeth explained what she needed, the receptionist responded,

"Doug is just walking past my desk, would you like to talk to him?" Elizabeth's thoughts began racing, *"It was 3:00 o'clock on Friday the day after Thanksgiving, Doug is leaving for a two-week trip to Hawaii, and he is still at the office. How could this be?"*

Joe's concern weighed on Elizabeth's mind, and she asked Doug about it. He explained a renal scan would be performed as part of the donor testing process to access the quality of her kidneys. Once all of the donor testing is completed, the collective results are reviewed, and the team verifies it's a "go" or "no go" with the donor.

Then nonchalantly Doug shared, *"Oh, we got the blood tests back and your blood and Mike's blood can cohabitate, you can be a donor."* Elizabeth's thoughts immediately went to her prayer request that God just answered. *"The donor would be identified by the end of November."*

Mike's two daughters were sitting on the bed next to her while she was on the phone and she whispered to them she could be a donor; they both broke down and cried tears of joy. Thanking Doug, Elizabeth hung up the phone and just sat on the bed hugging her nieces feeling excited, thrilled, and thankful. It was all coming together. Praise and thanksgiving to God were all Elizabeth could do. She couldn't wait to tell Mike. Susie came upstairs and Elizabeth shared the news. They embraced for a long time. They both knew they had just jumped over their first hurdle, now onto the second one, Mike agreeing to accept the kidney.

After returning to her home, Elizabeth felt frustrated and discouraged by her friend's and church group members' reactions to her becoming the donor. She was beyond excited, but as she tried to process her friend's concerns, she began to question herself, *"Did she miss something?"* Elizabeth did the only thing she knew to do to answer that question, she prayed a very simple direct prayer, *"Dear God, Am I to give my kidney to my brother? Amen"*

God answered Elizabeth's prayer the next day in a bible study she had been attending. Vicky, a member of the bible study, shared that God impressed upon her heart to read a specific scripture to answer one of the bible studies questions. She was confused, as the answer didn't seem to correlate with the question.

The minute Vicky began reading the scripture Elizabeth knew it was her answer to the prayer she had prayed the day before. She read 2 Corinthians 8:7-15,

"My opinion is that it is better for you to finish now what you began last year. You were the first, not only to act but also to be willing to act. On with it, then, and finish the job! Be as eager

to finish it, as you were to plan it, and do it with what you now have.

If you are eager to give, God will accept your gift on the basis of what you have to give, not on what you don't have. I am not trying to relieve others by putting a burden on you; but since you have plenty at this time, it is only fair that you should help those who are in need. Then, when you are in need and they have plenty, they will help you. In this way both are treated equally. As the scripture says, the one who gathered much did not have too much and the one who gathered little did not have too little."

Tears flowed down Elizabeth's face, warm, quiet, God-loving tears as Vicky continued reading the scripture. Elizabeth felt God embrace her warmly. How much more explicitly could God have answered her prayer?

When Elizabeth got home, she called Susie immediately and shared what she had just experienced. They both cried. Elizabeth told Susie, she had many prayers answered in her life, but few were so specific about how God would take care of her and confirmation that the journey they were experiencing was all part of His plan. Susie told Elizabeth to call Mike at work and tell him exactly what she had just shared with her.

Elizabeth called Mike and did just that. Mike was open to hearing what Elizabeth had just experienced. As she was reading the scripture to him, she heard him sniffle. After she finished, Mike became very quiet and then said, *"Well, I guess your kidney is going to be living in my body – whether I like it or not".* Elizabeth smiled and thought, *"God got Mike's attention and the second hurdle was just accomplished. Now to the finish line and winning the race!"*

Mike's health continued to deteriorate faster than anticipated. His feet began to swell, and he experienced extreme edema, which caused him to take an additional pair of socks and shoes to work, so he wouldn't come home with wet shoes and socks. He just felt awful and going to work began to really take a toll on his body, but Mike was determined to work as long as he could. He made an appointment with another Nephrologist regarding a shunt for dialysis thinking that dialysis may make him feel better.

The Nephrologist didn't agree with Mike's line of thinking, especially with the option of a kidney transplant right around the corner. This news discouraged Mike because he hadn't really accepted the gift that Elizabeth was giving.

The donor tests were completed by the middle of December and Elizabeth's Internist sent the results to Doug.

Anxiously waiting at home, Elizabeth prayed and stood in faith that Mike's health would hold out until a date for the kidney transplant could be confirmed. She prayed that Mike would go on God's dialysis if he needed relief.

During the final waiting period for the donor testing results, their brother Jack was preparing to become a donor if Elizabeth couldn't.

Christmas was nearing and there had not been word about the evaluation of Elizabeth's donor testing results. Still, Elizabeth stood in faith and knew she would be the donor, and everything was going to work out beautifully. Doug was returning from vacation and hopefully would expedite the donor evaluation and set a surgery date.

Elizabeth contacted Doug the day after he returned from Hawaii. Elizabeth asked what the next steps would be. Doug shared that Mike's insurance would need to be verified, plus Mike would be added to the surgical transplant list. The case would then be reviewed from both donor and recipient perspectives, and then a date for the surgery could be confirmed. He remembered that there were three dates available in January but needed to verify those.

Mike wanted Elizabeth to ask Doug about dialysis prior to the transplant because he was feeling so bad since there wasn't a date for the transplant yet. Doug's answer was an emphatic, *"NO, he definitely doesn't need to do that."* A prayer popped into Elizabeth's heart, *"God, plant a seed in Doug's mind that will let him know just how bad Mike feels and expedite the process to get a date for the transplant surgery."* Elizabeth felt the Lord telling her the surgery date would be known by the 20th of December. Elizabeth stood in faith and moved forward on that promise. In her heart, she was at peace and was able to leave everything in God's hands.

Starting to plan for the surgery, Mike and Elizabeth's parents wanted to help. They were coming to Chicago, and it was decided that their stepmom, Irene, would take care of Catie on the day of the surgery at Mike and Susie's home and John their Dad, would be with Mike and Elizabeth at the hospital. Knowing that Catie would be taken care of by Irene settled Elizabeth's heart. She knew they would have a great time together and Catie would be very well taken care of. When surgery day finally came, they made cookies, colored, and enjoyed a very special day together.

On December 18th the call finally came from Doug, Elizabeth was thrilled and couldn't be more excited. Doug had received the two remaining donor test results, evaluated them, and Elizabeth was officially approved by the medical center to donate her kidney. Elizabeth wanted to shout from the rooftops ... the finish line was close and they were entering the last lap of the race.

Doug shared the surgery schedule had an opening on Tuesday, the 12th of January, and asked Elizabeth if he should book it. With glee, Elizabeth told Doug to book it. Elizabeth prayed silently asking God to keep Mike going until the 12th of January so that he could receive one of the two gifts God had for him.

The week before the surgery, Elizabeth and Catie flew to Chicago. There was one final test that Elizabeth needed to complete prior to the surgery, a renal scan. Mike and Elizabeth's parents arrived in Chicago the same weekend and the family team was finally all together.

On Monday the 11th of January, Mike, Susie, Joe, and Elizabeth, drove to Northwestern Medical Center for pre-op testing and to meet with the kidney specialist Dr. Joe Leventhual. There was excitement in the air; chatting and laughter filled the car on the drive.

The pre-operative testing was standard, blood draw, urine sample, chest x-ray, and an electrocardiogram. Elizabeth also completed the renal scan, which was the last test needed for donor testing.

A DREAM COME TRUE

After the testing was completed, Dr. Leventhual shared that the surgery needed to be rescheduled due to an insurance issue. They had not been approved for the surgery. Mike and Elizabeth both just glared at the doctor. A look of discouragement came over both of them. Elizabeth thought to herself, *"What was going on? Why have we come this far only to have the process stopped? The insurance was approved already?"*

The ride home was very quiet. Elizabeth sat in the back seat and just prayed. *"Lord, what's up?"* A snowstorm had started that morning and as the snow continued to fall on the car windshield, it was like arrows penetrating Mike's heart. He was discouraged and at the point of just wanting this next hurdle to be over. Susie and Joe tried to make conversation with Mike and Elizabeth. But they weren't taking the bait. Elizabeth continued praying asking God for an answer. She knew in her heart the surgery would happen but wasn't sure when.

Due to the snowstorm, the drive back to Mike's house was a long two-and-half hours. Upon arriving home, dinner preparations began immediately. There was a house full of family and they needed to be fed. Everyone seemed to feel the tension in the air, but there wasn't anything that could be done to resolve it immediately. So once the food was ready, they gathered at the table, prayed, and ate.

104

Around 9:00 p.m. the phone rang, it was the medical center, the insurance was approved, and the surgery was rescheduled for Thursday the 14th. That was good news and all God!!

Thankfully, the medical center provided accommodations for Elizabeth and Mike, and their spouses the night before the surgery, since they had to arrive at the medical center at 4:00 a.m. They spent the night in downtown Chicago, had dinner out, prayed together, and then left for their respective apartments only to meet up very early the following morning.

Elizabeth had trouble sleeping. The "green frog" cocktail required to drink prior to surgery kept her up and down all night. It really didn't matter if she slept that night, she would surely be sleeping after the surgery. 4:00 a.m. came quickly. Walking to the hospital was frigid. They were only two blocks away, but the wind that whipped off Lake Michigan was bitter cold. The stillness of the dark night was beautiful, the reflective moonlight against the newly fallen snow made Elizabeth stop and thank God for the powerful journey she and Mike had walked through. Only God could have orchestrated the entire excursion, and they hadn't made it to the finish line yet. The admissions process was simple and quick, and Elizabeth didn't have much recollection of it.

She was taken to surgery first at 6:30 a.m. In the pre-op room, a nurse came to talk to Elizabeth prior to the surgery. Her piercing eyes showed such love. The way she held her hand and the calming words spoken brought a peace that Elizabeth felt from the top of her head to the tip of her toes. Elizabeth pondered on the thought she was an angel sent by God.

Elizabeth shared that her brother, Mike, would be coming down next. The nurse assured her everything was going to be fine and she would be visiting him as well. After receiving the first shot, Elizabeth didn't remember anything until waking up in her hospital room. Joe looked very concerned and was extremely silent. He let Elizabeth sleep, thinking to himself, *"You look like you've just been in a fight. I've been through ten surgeries with you, and you've never looked this bad, so swollen and bruised."* Joe stayed by Elizabeth's side.

Mike was taken down for surgery at 11:00 a.m. As he was waiting in the pre-operative area, the same nurse came to see him that visited Elizabeth. Mike remembered her piercing eyes too and how comforted he felt in her presence. The surgery went as planned. Elizabeth had two very large kidneys and the one Mike received fit perfectly and functioned immediately. Only God could have orchestrated this entire plan.

After a couple of days, both Elizabeth and Mike were discharged and returned to Mike's house to recuperate. A highlight of their day was spending the mornings together sharing and reading the day's mail. During one of those mornings, Mike said to Elizabeth, *"You know this experience wasn't about my kidney, don't you?"* Elizabeth's response was, *"What do you think it was about?"* Mike shared, *"It was about your obedience to God".* Elizabeth just soaked in what she had just heard; thanking God that Mike could see this and that God had touched him in a miraculous way.

Elizabeth asked Mike what his deciding factor was, which allowed him to totally surrender and accept the gift that God was giving him. Mike shared, *"When you called me at the office the day God answered your prayer in bible study."*

In Elizabeth's heart, she knew she walked a journey that only God could have orchestrated. God had planted the seed in her early teens that if Mike needed a kidney, she would give him her extra one. She had to laugh when they found out that she had two large kidneys and a small bladder. So many miracles along the way, the timing, the people, and the layout of the plan, so many of the details were addressed before they became issues. Throughout the entire journey, God's hand was ever-present down to the most finite detail. How could anyone ever doubt that?

Only God could do that. As Elizabeth pondered all that had happened, her next thought was, so Lord, what's the next challenge?

--TAKE AWAY--

- Give of yourself – be a servant to others and obey God.

1 Peter 4:10 *"God has given each of you a gift from his great variety of spiritual gifts. Use them well to serve one another."*

Philippians 4:13 *"For I can do everything through Christ, who gives me strength."*

Mark 10:45 *"For even the Son of Man came not to be served but to serve others and to give his life as a ransom for many."*

Serve in love – patiently, kindly, not easily angered, and unselfishly as it tells us in the Love Chapter of the Bible (1 Corinthians 13). Love is the action. It doesn't matter how much talent you have. What matters is that you are willing to use it to serve others. Jesus' motive for ministry was to serve not to be served.

PART IV: PERSEVERANCE AND REWARD

Chapter 7 - Who Would Have Thought?

Catie was three years old and the desire to have another baby lingered in Elizabeth's heart, if it was to happen, only God could orchestrate it. She and Joe were beyond the age limits required for adoption, and there wasn't any other way to have a baby.

Elizabeth's thoughts lingered on how hard it would be for Catie to care for elderly parents being an only child. She would have her hands full. Joe and Elizabeth were older when they became parents, and the responsibility could be overwhelming. She prayed and asked God to either change the desire of her heart or grant a miracle with a second child to complement their family. Elizabeth had first-hand experience with miracles up to this point in her life, and she knew it could happen.

Healing from the donor surgery seemed like the recovery process was taking a little longer this time, or maybe she was just impatient. After eleven surgeries she knew the process well, she was no amateur! Thankfully, Catie and Elizabeth would play together in the mornings and nap in the afternoons, which Elizabeth looked forward to.

As the months wore on, the answer to her prayer didn't seem apparent. Elizabeth didn't give up hope but found peace in her daily devotions and held tight knowing God heard her prayer. She knew in His time God would answer her. Having learned through experience, God answers our prayers, but not always in our timing or the timing may not be right for all parties, Elizabeth moved forward in her faith even though it wasn't always easy to understand.

On the morning of June 22nd, as Elizabeth was having her devotion time, she felt the Holy Spirit guide her to chapter 4 in 2 Kings in the Bible. It is the story of Elisha, who visited the town of Shunem. A well-to-do Shunammite woman was there who urged Elisha to have a meal with her and her husband, which he did. The woman knew Elisha was a holy man of God and suggested to her husband they make a small room on the roof where he could stay whenever he came to Shunem.

Each time Elisha came to Shunem he stayed with them. Elisha was very thankful for the accommodations, and he asked his servant to call the Shunammite woman and ask, *"You have gone to all this trouble for us, what can be done for you?"* The woman answered, *"I have a home among my own people"*, then Elisha's servant said, *"She has no son, and her husband is old."* Then

Elisha said, *"About this time next year you will hold a son in your arms."*

The woman responded, *"No my Lord, please, man of God, don't mislead your servant."* But the woman became pregnant, and the next year about that same time she gave birth to a son, just as Elisha had told her.

As Elizabeth read, the verses leaped off the page, and into her heart, she soared with joy. That was her answer. God was giving it to her in his word. She responded out loud, *"God, I'm holding you to that."* Elizabeth's thoughts continued, *"Great, I have a year to plan for a son to complete our family"*. Praise God from whom all blessings flow the desires of her heart would soon be coming to fruition.

Elizabeth shared with Joe that evening her devotion and the verses God laid on her heart. Joe's reaction was understated, and he said, *"I wouldn't be surprised if it happens, and I won't be surprised if it doesn't happen."* He was kind, reserved, and calm.

Elizabeth thought since the birth of their son was coming in a year; she had plenty of time for preparation and to help transition Catie into becoming a big sister. Excited and thrilled, Elizabeth shared the news with her best friend Judy. Not only had Judy adopted her son, but she also had a giant faith in God and stood next to Elizabeth as they prayed this child into Elizabeth and Joe's family.

On a Sunday morning in August, as Elizabeth was walking down a flight of stairs Julie, a friend of Elizabeth's, asked if she and Joe would be open to adopting another child. Julie was on the board of an adoption agency and one of their birth mothers' birth plans had been rescinded with the couple she had selected. Cher, the birth mother, was devastated upon hearing the news that the selected adoptive parents could no longer accept her baby. The adoption staff and board were trying to assist Cher with creating a new birth plan.

As Julie was sharing, and people were passing them, Elizabeth felt light-headed and her thoughts went to the scripture God had given her two months earlier in June, 2 Kings 4:16 *"You will hold a son in your arms next year,"* Elizabeth thought, *"Lord is this the one?"* Her response to Julie was quick and immediate, *"Yes, but I'll need to talk with Joe and let you know tomorrow".* After arriving home and having lunch, Joe and Elizabeth sat down to talk about the new opportunity that had been placed on their lap. Joe gave a solid green "go" light and needless to say Elizabeth just kept thinking about 2 Kings 4:16. Thanking God for this miracle, not knowing how it would unfold but believing God was in control. Her stomach fluttered and joy filled her heart.

The next day Elizabeth contacted Julie with excitement. She shared that she and Joe were open to adopting another baby and asked what the next step would be.

Julie shared the birth mother's story. She had built a close relationship with the previously selected adoptive parents and her world was devastated when the adoptive parents found out they were pregnant and rescinded their agreement. Cher didn't really want to place the baby for adoption in the first place. Then to have her birth plan rescinded after building a good relationship with the adoptive parents left Cher feeling, rejected, hopeless, and overwhelmed. To begin the process all over again was going to be exhaustive and Cher really didn't have the energy to do it or the time.

Joe and Elizabeth were excited about the adoption and knew that Cher was due in late August or early September, just eight weeks away. They understood that the typical process for adoption was obviously not going to be followed. During this time,

Elizabeth and Joe were working together at their firm, and they began receiving mail for another company. Coincidently, it was for the adoption agency across the street from their office. Elizabeth understood the mail sometimes is delivered to the wrong place, but after reading the name of the agency, her thoughts trailed to Julie. The agency she was a board member of, was the agency their firm was receiving mail for.

Elizabeth felt sure this was from God! After receiving their mail all week, Elizabeth knew she needed to go over, introduce herself, and give them their mail.

Julie had spoken with the Agency's Executive Director, Debbie, and shared that she had attended a bible study with Elizabeth through the kidney transplant and experienced first-hand all the miracles and moments of that journey. She assured Debbie that Joe and Elizabeth were thrilled about the opportunity to adopt again and solid people. Debbie had been counseling Cher and knew her heart. She suggested to Julie to have Joe and Elizabeth make an appointment with her.

Joe and Elizabeth had not heard anything from Julie or the agency, since their original conversation. Their last knowledge of any activity was that the agency was trying to reach Cher to discuss the option with her. She had not attended her last therapy appointment and wasn't responding to any of their calls.

The entire situation was completely up in the air. As Elizabeth waited for answers, she soon realized this process would become the norm, and it was grueling.

Elizabeth finally went over to the agency, introduced herself, and gave the mail to Shari, the administrative assistant. Then she asked to speak with Debbie. Shari shared Debbie was in a meeting and not available. Elizabeth was disappointed but understood she hadn't made an appointment to see Debbie. Just as Elizabeth was leaving, Debbie stepped out of her meeting and asked Shari a question. Shari stopped Elizabeth from leaving and introduced her to Debbie, referencing who she was in regard to Cher. Debbie asked her, *"If Cher were to have her son today are you ready to move forward?"* Elizabeth's thoughts went immediately to the scripture verse God gave her; *"You will hold a son in your arms at the same time next year"*.

"A son, yes Lord, a son." She knew she needed to answer Debbie but was lost in her thoughts 2 Kings 4:16. Every detail was coming true, only God, thank you Lord was on Elizabeth's lips. She then responded to Debbie, *"Yes, we are ready"*. Debbie explained that they were trying to reach Cher and not having any luck, she reassured Elizabeth that they would continue and then slipped back into her meeting.

Elizabeth left the adoption office floating on a puffy white cloud. In her mind she kept repeating 2 Kings 4:16. Her heart was filled with so much excitement and gratefulness. Once back at the office, Elizabeth shared the news with Joe. He smiled and said, *"Let's just see how this all unfolds"*.

August moved slowly, they still had not heard from the agency regarding Cher's decision. Always in the forefront of her mind, Elizabeth asked God, *"Is this to be my son, how should I pray?"* She always prayed for the baby's health and stood in faith that God was going to follow through on His promise through scripture.

But to be honest, Elizabeth thought God wasn't moving fast enough for her.

One morning while having devotions, Elizabeth felt God laid Cher on her heart with the need to pray. The need was so strong, an intense feeling came over her and she felt despair all throughout her body. A sadness that was deep and forceful. She cried out to God in desperation and lifted Cher up, claiming scripture to help her fight whatever spiritual battle she was in. Elizabeth personalized her favorite verse for Cher, *"No weapon formed against Cher will proposer in Jesus' Name."* Elizabeth lay on the floor in a cross position and wailed. She wept long and hard and was exhausted after she got up.

In her quiet time, Elizabeth shared with God that if the only reason she and Joe were brought into Cher's life was to pray for her through the pregnancy that was fine. She would take it on as an assignment. Her heart was full of love for Cher, who seemed to be so lost in thinking that her only option was to place the child she had carried, loved, and nurtured for nine months … away.

Even though Elizabeth was on the other side of the coin, she couldn't imagine what it would be like to place a child. Elizabeth's joy of having a child would be such a high price for Cher to pay. Probably like ripping your arm off. Elizabeth grieved and cried heavy tears for everything that Cher experienced. Her heart became very tender towards her.

For the next seven days, Elizabeth interceded with prayer on Cher's behalf. She had never prayed for someone this hard and with such intensity, at times travailing for her. On the eighth day, Elizabeth asked God, *"What else can I do?* "And she felt God say, … *"Rest in me, Elizabeth."*

The following day, Debbie contacted Elizabeth with the news that Cher had called and was ready to place her child. Debbie was going to share with Cher that she had met Elizabeth and Joe and asked if Cher was open to scheduling an appointment for Monday, so they could all meet.

Joe had dental surgery on that Monday, but they still met. Cher wanted to meet Joe, Elizabeth, and Catie together as a family to learn how they interacted with each other. Her heart wasn't really in any of it, but she knew she had to move forward with some sort of plan for her baby. The meeting went well, Joe was not feeling 100% and Elizabeth prayed asking God to bring peace to all who were attending. Catie played quietly on the floor or sat in Elizabeth's lap. Cher asked many questions and Joe and Elizabeth answered them as best as they could. They didn't have a chance to create a life book, per agency protocol, due to time constraints and a decision not being made, so they shared their story as best they could.

Cher looked so tired and very pregnant, and the desire to keep her baby was very evident. Just as the numbing medication was wearing off and Joe started to feel the pain of the procedure, the meeting came to a close.

After the meeting, Joe and Elizabeth didn't know what Cher was thinking. Debbie walked out with them and said she'd be in contact. Elizabeth knew in her heart, that if this were the child God had for them, everything would work out. She had to stand firm in her faith. God had given her a promise of a son that she would hold in her arms the same time next year, and she believed He would fulfill that promise.

Joe returned to the office and Elizabeth and Catie went home. Being three years old, Catie didn't know what was happening and how her world was going to change. Elizabeth felt the need to begin preparing Catie, but she wanted to do it carefully

120

and at a level that Catie would understand. They were swinging together in the play gym in the backyard together and Elizabeth asked Catie, *"What do you think it would be like to have a brother?"* Catie thought for a moment and then said, "Fine, I could play with him, we'd be just like Baily and Garrett". Elizabeth shared, *"That's right, honey"*.

Baily was a friend Catie had met in gymnastics who had a baby brother born in July. They were both adopted, and God formed their family in a miraculous way. The girls happened to be born on the same day and enjoyed playing together outside of gymnastics. Elizabeth was thrilled that Catie related to another family that had just experienced a joyful occasion. Catie's life was going to change drastically, and the anticipation seemed to be met with open arms.

Elizabeth had shared with Carolyn, Baily, and Garrett's Mom how the events of having another child were unfolding. The desire in Elizabeth's heart, the scripture revelation, and the meeting of Cher. Carolyn knew all too well the process of infertility, heartache, and the joy of having two adopted children. She was a very kind person, and Elizabeth appreciated her friendship.

Finally, a call came from Debbie. Elizabeth's thoughts were racing back and forth. What did Cher decide? How is she? Is

121

the baby, okay? She wanted to know everything but needed to calm down so she could hear what Debbie was saying. Cher thought Elizabeth and Joe would be acceptable parents for the baby. She really liked Catie and thought she was cute. She pictured her son with Catie playing and having fun. She wanted to pray about the entire situation before she made a final decision.

Time seemed to move at a snail's pace and again Cher seemed to have gone into hiding. She was not attending her therapy sessions, per agency requirements, nor answering calls. It seemed she just wanted to check out of reality. Joe and Elizabeth were told to just continue on with their life like nothing had changed in their daily routine. This did not come easily to Elizabeth. God had given her an answer to prayer through scripture and she wasn't giving up.

August turned into September and still, Joe and Elizabeth heard nothing. By this time Catie was asking about her possible brother, and all Elizabeth could say to her was, *"If Cher's baby is the brother God has for us, He will bless us with him"*. It broke Elizabeth's heart but Catie seemed to be okay with the answer until she would ask again.

Friday night of Labor Day weekend ensued, and no plans were scheduled, but Joe's alma mater was scheduled to play football. With his parents living in the same city as his alma mater,

Joe and Elizabeth thought they might go to the football game to keep the focus on something other than "the baby" and spend the night with his parents. Catie's girlfriend, Keily was over for the night. Her parents were celebrating their anniversary and the girls were having a sleepover. Elizabeth called Keily's Mom, Leisha, to make sure it was okay to take Keily to the game, Keily's Dad did not want her to leave the city. Elizabeth and Leisha both thought that was odd but acquiesced to his concern. They ended up watching the football game on TV, while the girls played dress-up and stayed busy.

Saturday morning, Elizabeth called Leisha to arrange for a delayed pickup of Keily. The girls wanted to play a bit longer than originally scheduled. During the phone conversation, Leisha asked if they had heard anything about the baby, to which Elizabeth said, *"No"*. The hospital where Cher was delivering her baby was just blocks from their home, but Elizabeth knew she wouldn't be able to obtain any information based on HIPPA rules. In fact, the baby could have already been born and she had decided to keep him. Leisha responded, *"Well I'll just call to verify that she is a patient, I'm not one to take no for an answer"*. Elizabeth responded with, *"If you want to call fine, but please call me back if you obtain any new news."*

So, Leisha called the hospital and then called Elizabeth back. She found out Cher was there and in labor. Elizabeth

123

wondered how she obtained the information. But she never asked because she was afraid of the answer. She was just thankful they knew something.

Elizabeth called Debbie and shared the news. Cher had not notified Debbie regarding anything, which was agency protocol, her decision, or the fact that she was in labor and at the hospital. Debbie contacted the hospital to find out the details and spoke with Cher. Everyone had been waiting for Cher's decision. She told Debbie that Joe and Elizabeth could come to the hospital and if she was going to place her son, it would be with them. It was obvious to Debbie that wasn't her final decision.

Debbie called Elizabeth back and shared the news. Elizabeth was reserved in her response; nothing was affirmed, and everything was still up in the air. So, they could be going up for nothing, and then God reminded Elizabeth of what she had shared with Him. *"Even if praying for Cher was the only reason, they walked this journey she would do it".* Elizabeth's thoughts lingered, *"Yes, I hear you, Lord, thank you, I will try my best to honor what I said."*

After dinner, Joe, Elizabeth, and Catie went up to the hospital. Debbie was going to meet them at the hospital in the labor and delivery waiting room. They arrived first, but it wasn't long before Debbie met up with them. Debbie shared that the baby had been born at 7:05 p.m. that evening. Cher wasn't doing too well but was with a good friend of hers named Elizabeth. Joe and Elizabeth were then told that they could see the baby through the screening window in labor and delivery.

Cher's parents were also at the hospital, and together they all waited with excitement and great anticipation to meet that sweet baby boy. As they were standing at the window, Cher's Mom, Kathy was standing next to Elizabeth and Catie, and Cher's Dad, Ed was standing next to Joe on the other side of the window, each of them began to share how inattentive parents they were to Cher and all their children. How they had let their children do as they pleased and the way they dealt with situations during their upbringing that they weren't proud of.

Elizabeth really didn't want to hear any of their stories, nor did she want Catie to either. She didn't want to seem unkind, but their guilt and sorrow weren't something she could process when she was meeting her son.

In Elizabeth's heart, as she looked at that sweet, dreamy boy – he was her son. The one God had created for her and Joe. The son she would hold in her arms the same time next year – just like the scripture stated, their son and Catie's brother. As they watched their newborn, Elizabeth noticed how grey he looked, and he was really struggling to breathe. One nurse was holding him, and another had an oxygen tube very near his nose and mouth. They didn't stay long at the window; in fact, they seemed to have whisked him away pretty quickly.

Elizabeth asked Debbie what was wrong with the baby, and she shared she didn't know. She thought he looked beautiful. Elizabeth knew something was up, she could feel it in her spirit. Debbie told Elizabeth she and Joe should go home and wait for the call tomorrow to come and pick up their son. If Cher were going to place him, they would be his parents.

They left the hospital with reserved excitement that their son was born, and he would be coming home with them the following day. Elizabeth called her Dad and shared the news. Sadly, she couldn't answer any of his questions because she didn't have any answers. She continued to respond with, *"I don't know"*. The one thing they did know was their son's name. Elizabeth had always loved the name Elliott – which means, *"The Lord is my God"* and she wanted it to be part of his full name. Since their son was scripture birthed, she and Joe both agreed on it. His full name would be James Elliott Michael, after two of his uncles and he would be called Elliott.

God had orchestrated this entire plan and Elizabeth knew he would fulfill what He started even if she had no idea how and when. She knew she had to stand in faith and not waiver, and she wanted to with all her heart, but she just wanted to know that on

Sunday she would be bringing her son home to live with them, and they would live "happily ever after".

But would it be? Was this the child that God had for them?

--TAKE AWAY--

- God's Plan for your life is often much bigger than you realize.

Psalm 37:3-7 "Trust in the Lord and do good. Then you will live safely in the land and prosper. Take delight in the Lord and he will give you your heart's desire. Commit everything you do to the Lord. Trust Him, and he will help you. He will make your innocence radiate like the dawn, and the justice of your cause will shine like the noonday sun. Be still in the presence of the Lord and wait patiently for him to act. Don't worry about evil people who prosper or fret about their wicked schemes."

2 Corinthians 1:3-4 "Blessed be the God and Father of our Lord Jesus Christ, the Father of mercies and the God of all comfort. He comforts us in all our affliction, so that we may be able to comfort those who are in any kind of affliction, through the comfort we ourselves receive from God."

We are called to take delight in the Lord and to commit everything we have and do to Him. To experience great pleasure and joy in God's presence, we must know Him better. Trust in Him, believing that He can care for us better than we can ourselves. Often, someone in the Bible typically has already experienced an example of what you are experiencing. Seeking

God in his word and experiencing Him assures us of His love for us. As you pursue your relationship with God, situations occur that can be indicators of change, when we follow God's leading. God is good, faithful, and trustworthy.

When we follow God's direction, we will witness things happening in our lives that can only be explained by His powerful presence. God will use our experiences of receiving His comfort when we share the comfort we have received from God with others. He is the Father of mercies and God of all comfort.

A DREAM COME TRUE

Chapter 8 – Faith Beyond

Labor Day weekend brought intense internal turmoil for Elizabeth. The memory that was being etched into her heart wouldn't ever be easy to relive -*"Lord say it isn't so, please?"*

On Sunday after church, Keily came over and gave Catie a gift that every big sister needed, a "Big Sister shirt". They were both excited and Keily kept asking, *"When is he coming? When is he coming? I want to meet Elliott."* In Elizabeth's heart she asked the same question, *"When is Elliott coming home to live with us?"*

The girls helped Elizabeth prepare Elliott's cradle and dresser. They each placed a small stuffed animal in his cradle and helped assemble the mobile, which hung above it. Preparing for his homecoming was fun even though Elizabeth guarded her heart, she wondered when it would happen.

The day lagged on, and Joe and Elizabeth waited for the call from Cher, but it never came. In the late afternoon, Elizabeth was struggling and couldn't wait any longer, she called the hospital, and Cher's sister, Theresa, answered the phone. Theresa shared Cher was sick and wasn't accepting any visitors or taking calls. She then explained what was happening, and as she spoke

Elizabeth felt like her heart was torn in two and beat almost to a crawl. *"No Lord, say it isn't so."*

Elliott was gravely ill. Cher had a bladder infection and during delivery, Elliott was exposed to bacteria in the birth canal. Having just given birth Cher was in pain and exhausted. Elliott was in Pediatric Intensive Care Unit (PICU) with neonatal sepsis. His white blood count was dangerously high, he had a fever, and a rapid heart rate, and the distress from delivery affected his condition. Elizabeth reflected on when she first saw Elliott and how labored his breathing was, plus the oxygen tube held so close to his face. He looked grey, beautiful, but grey. Theresa said he wasn't doing well at all, and they didn't know what the outcome would be, life or death. She assured Elizabeth that they would keep her up to date on his condition, but there wasn't anything else to tell her.

Elizabeth hung up the phone and slumped down into the chair next to her. She was trying to process everything she had just heard but struggled. Really struggled. This wasn't how she expected her son's birth and entry into the world to unfold. Not prepared to handle any of this, she went to Joe and the minute he saw Elizabeth's face he knew it wasn't good. Her body language screamed devastation. Her dream was crushing right before her eyes, and she knew she had to hold fast. She fell into Joe's arms

132

and tried to explain everything she had just heard calmly, but the tears wouldn't stop and Joe couldn't understand her. Their sweet baby boy was in a sterile hospital with tubes in and out of his body, monitors flashing and no one was comforting him, holding and loving him, reassuring him that God would be faithful. Elizabeth wept and her arms ached from not being able to hold him. Joe calmly shared that everything would work out, and Elizabeth's thoughts went immediately to how different they each processed pain and hurt differently. For her, this was not a time for logic but for action through the only avenue available to them – PRAYER.

Elizabeth contacted her dear friend Elizabeth W. in the early evening. She had always been a spiritual mentor in her life. Brokenhearted Elizabeth poured out the latest news she had received about Elliott and how desperate the situation seemed.

Elizabeth W. spoke like a prophetess, she directed Joe and Elizabeth to pray over Elliott, stand in the gap for him, take a position of authority as his parents, and claim victory over his life on the basis of God's word that He gave us through scripture. Claim healing over his high blood count and cover Elliott with the blood of Jesus Christ from the top of his head to the base of his soles. Plead Elliott's case before the Lord, cast out demons, and fight for their son. Speak life over Elliott not death, stand in protection, and speak to his immune system. Petition that no weapon formed against him will prosper in Jesus' name, that Elliott is healed and whole by the blood of the Lamb.

And Joe and Elizabeth did just that. Praying together like this wasn't something they had ever done before. But they knew it was not a time to question but to act.

Elliott was in limbo between his life in the womb and his new life with Joe and Elizabeth. They needed to fight for him in the spirit. Praying together to claim victory for their son. Sunday night dragged on, it was sad and very quiet.

Monday was Labor Day and upon waking Elizabeth was hit by the reality of the circumstances. Joe went to work taking advantage of the holiday and working without interruption to get a good start on the week. Elizabeth started doing laundry, and the pile of ironing staring at her was going to be the project for the day. Ironing was a calming activity for her. To take a wrinkled piece of clothing and turn it into a crisp pressed, ready-to-wear article wasn't something everyone knew how to do. Her friends would tease her about it, but she loved the way it looked once pressed.

The day ensued and Elizabeth still waited for a phone call. Her thoughts continued to taunt her; *"Cher could have left the hospital by now. Elliott would be laying up in PICU all alone. You can't even go up there."* This broke Elizabeth's heart and tears streamed down her face as she ironed and ironed and ironed.

The morning turned into afternoon, and the longer Elizabeth ironed the more she felt burdened and beaten up with the whole situation and circumstances surrounding it. *"What was Cher thinking? Could she be this mean? Was she not thinking about anyone else?"* The more Elizabeth thought about it, the more intense her feelings became.

She stopped ironing and called Debbie. She poured out her feelings and was totally taken aback by Debbie's response, *"You just need to pick up the pieces and go on with life, we don't know what Cher is going to do, it is her decision, and we have no control over it. Just move on."*

Elizabeth wanted to explode. Her body was tense, and her head pounded. Her heart had literally been ripped in two. How could this be happening? Her emotions totally took over her mind and she was ravaged. Thinking wasn't an option only acting and she didn't like what was happening. She had no control over anything.

She went to Catie, picked her up, and held her in her arms. Her heart was pounding fast. She began pouring out her love for her sweet, beautiful daughter, *"Mommy loves you so much Catie, you are very special to me I am so thankful you are in my life."* Elizabeth just cried intensely and Catie didn't understand what was wrong. *"What's wrong Mommy?"* she asked. Elizabeth told her she had just heard the sad news and needed a hug from her. Catie graciously and with great effort hugged Elizabeth and patted her on her back, then told her she loved her and it would be all right.

Elizabeth didn't know what to do. She was so caught up in her emotions. She just knew she needed to do something! So, she asked Catie if she would like to take their neighbors to the spray pool at the park. Catie responded cheerfully, *"Oh yes Mommy, let's go"*. Elizabeth contacted her neighbors and the children piled into Elizabeth's car and off they went to the park. Elizabeth had to get out of the house. She needed to feel the fresh hot summer air and experience something different than the dread and anger she felt inside. They all got wet and started to chase each other. The children seemed to really enjoy it, laughter and screams of joy - but Elizabeth continued feeling dread and fear even though she was soaking wet too.

Joe called while they were at the park to see how things were going. He didn't know what kind of day Elizabeth had or if she had heard anything from Cher or Debbie. Elizabeth was very tentative on the phone and Joe picked up on it. Joe continued to ask questions and when Elizabeth finally opened her heart and exposed her raw feelings, Joe asked where she was. He asked Elizabeth to stay there; he was coming to the park and would leave immediately.

Catie was thrilled to see her Daddy at the park, and Joe greeted her warmly. He asked Elizabeth to join him on the park bench near the spray pool. Elizabeth couldn't get her head around what was happening. She told Joe exactly how she felt, poured her heart out and just cried angry painful tears. The pain and agony of being strung along just to be told, *"No I'm taking your son and raising him, giving him up is too much to bear"*. It was too much for Elizabeth to process let alone hear.

Joe tried to console Elizabeth, he shared that he knew Cher wasn't doing this on purpose. She was torn herself. How could she give up her baby? At the moment Elizabeth couldn't put herself in Cher's shoes, she was hurting too bad herself. To come so far so close to having another child, to have that just taken away so abruptly. Joe was trying to console Elizabeth, but they weren't on the same page. Elizabeth needed empathy and Joe was sharing logic. It was like they were on the same highway, just not in the same car, a mirrored image of their marriage. Joe tried again, *"This isn't over yet, Elizabeth, Elliott is still in the hospital. Nothing has been settled."* Elizabeth struggled intensely with his reaction to the situation.

After talking for quite a while, Joe suggested they round up the children and take them home. He offered to make dinner. After Elizabeth put Catie to bed, Joe noticed how exhausted she was and suggested that he sleep in the spare room. This would allow Elizabeth to enjoy a hot bath with soft music and then go to bed whenever. Elizabeth appreciated Joe's thoughtfulness, but she didn't think anything would cheer her up or take the numbness from her heart. It was too heavy, sad, and hopeless. Her son was in immediate danger, and she couldn't do a thing. Not even comfort him.

After her bath, she crawled into bed and just lay there. She knew God had given her an answer to her prayer in June, with 2 Kings 4:16, but she also remembered committing to stand by Cher if that was the only reason, they had met. *"Lord, which was it?"*

Finally, Elizabeth fell into a deep sleep and was startled when awoken abruptly at 2:00 a.m. She jumped out of bed and felt a power come over her that was strong and passionately severe. Something she hadn't experienced before. She started to pray with a ferocious passion, claiming victory over Elliott's health and well-being. Calling on the scripture that God gave her (2 Kings 4:16) and taking authority against the devil, she had the power. Elizabeth persevered, continuing the fight over this battle, praising, singing, and claiming the victory of life not death for her son Elliott.

Quoting scripture after scripture authoritatively. This continued for about two hours. When she stopped, she shouted out loud, *"It is finished"*. Elizabeth was exhausted. Her body felt like she had been in an intense physical battle and bore the bruises to prove it. She fell back onto the bed as a limp piece of clothing and fell into a deep sleep.

In the morning she awoke with a joy in her heart that could only have been explained by God, the peace that passes all understanding. Elizabeth knew in her heart and spirit that everything was going to be all right. The battle had been won. Elizabeth knew God had them all in the palm of His hands and remembered that it's not you the enemy is afraid of; it's God's spirit within you.

Catie slept in and Elizabeth enjoyed a sweet devotional time and praised God for the peace welling up inside of her. Debbie called Elizabeth, and upon hearing her voice, she said, *"You sound like a different person"*, and Elizabeth's response was, *"I am!"*

Elizabeth began to share with Debbie the encounter with God she had experienced during the night. Debbie listened attentively and after she finished, she shared in awe what she also experienced that night. God had awakened Debbie at 2:00 a.m. and shared that she needed to fight in the spirit for Elliott. So, Debbie did. Tears came streaming down Elizabeth's face as she listened with intensity. Only God could have orchestrated Elliott's homecoming, not anyone else. Together, these women had fought the fight and God gave them both a powerful peace about the outcome.

As the morning ensued, Catie and Elizabeth thought a day with Baily and Carolyn would be fun. So, they packed their bags and off they went. The day was filled with laughter, as the girls played in ear reach, Carolyn and Elizabeth were scrapbooking and having an entertaining time themselves as they shared stories of the memories they were placing in their scrapbooks.

The day was light and went by fairly quickly before they knew it was time to go home. Thankful for the day, as Elizabeth was making dinner, she was talking with her friend Leisha on the phone. Simultaneously, Debbie was trying to contact Elizabeth on the phone with the news she had been waiting for. She had even thought of calling the phone company to have them break into Elizabeth's phone call.

Cher had contacted Debbie early that morning, and they met during the day. She had made the decision to place Elliott with Joe and Elizabeth. Debbie wanted Elizabeth to come and pick up the signed guardianship papers.

It was rush hour and Debbie lived south of the city, coming from downtown the traffic would be gridlocked, but Elizabeth jumped at the chance of picking up the guardianship documentation. She and Catie sprang to the car and drove to Debbie's house. *"Finally,"* Elizabeth thought, *"He is ours"* not knowing the next hurdle that they'd be facing.

Home from Debbie's, Joe, Elizabeth, and Catie sat down and tried to eat dinner while talking about going to meet Elliott. Catie shared that she wanted to dress up and look her best. She was anxious to meet her brother. It had been raining and the rain turned into an intense storm with thunder and lightning.

Off to the hospital, Joe, Elizabeth, and Catie walked with a hint of excitement in their step. Elizabeth's thoughts relived the last six weeks, her emotions followed the path of a roller coaster, and she was looking forward to getting off the ride.

They arrived at the Pediatric Intensive Care Unit (PICU) with great enthusiasm and joy Elizabeth went in to meet her sweet baby boy, Elliott. A nurse abruptly stopped her and as Elizabeth began sharing why she was there a very puzzled look and frown formed on the nurse's face. The nurse knew who Cher was, but nothing about adoption had been discussed and Cher had been there all that day. In fact, Cher had asked about breastfeeding the baby and other at-home care instructions. Elizabeth felt a strong

141

resistance from the nurse, guardianship papers or no guardianship papers Elizabeth prayed, *"Please Lord give me great favor with this nurse. Help me communicate with love and grace and allow this woman to accept it and let me meet my son. He is so close to me I'll die if I can't see him, please Lord."*

The nurse reviewed the guardianship papers and then conferred with another nurse. She couldn't believe that Cher was going to place this child after all that was discussed that day.

It seemed like the nurses had been talking forever, Elizabeth wanted to meet her son, touch him, share with him how much she loved him and would take the very best care of him. Finally, the nurse came back to Elizabeth and said, *"Well, since you have guardianship papers, I guess we legally have to let you see him, but this doesn't make any sense."* Elizabeth didn't appreciate her response or the tone of her delivery but understood she was doing her job and she was thrilled to be escorted to finally meet Elliott.

Elliott lay in his crib, hooked to what seemed like a million tubes going into his head, mouth, and hands along with a nasal cannula for oxygen. The machines were making so much noise surrounding his little crib. Elizabeth touched him and the nurse rebuked her. *"Don't touch him, he is very sensitive and gets irritated when touched".* She felt like a teacher was scolding her.

142

In Elizabeth's mind, she wanted to tell the nurse a thing or two but kept quiet.

Elizabeth asked the nurse a myriad of questions regarding Elliott's condition. *"What was actually wrong with him? What progress was he making? What the road ahead looked like?"* The nurse shared that when he was admitted, he had neonatal sepsis, an infection that was passed at birth, and his body response was extreme. Without timely treatment, sepsis can rapidly lead to tissue damage, organ failure, and death.

The nurse continued sharing the glaring facts about sepsis and Elizabeth didn't really want to hear them because God was going to heal her precious son. The nurse went on to say, it typically strikes the very old and the very young. Children, particularly newborns and young infants, can be more susceptible to developing sepsis and statistically children die from sepsis more often than from cancer.

The PICC (Peripherally Inserted Central Catheter) inserted in Elliott's head was something Elizabeth had never seen before and as the nurse was spouting off statistics, she also shared that PICCs are used to administer medication in infants and children that need IV fluids or medicine over long periods of time, which Elliott would. A small soft tube was inserted through a vein in his head until it reached a large vein near the heart. The PICC can stay in for two to three weeks or longer.

This all seemed so matter-of-fact to the nurse, she continued sharing that Elliott wasn't eating and the medication was working but not like they had hoped. But in the middle of last night, he had a real turnaround, his stats began changing and it looked like he was making a comeback. That afternoon he ate more than he had since being admitted.

Elizabeth thought of the 2:00 a.m. prayers and how God honored them, she and Debbie claimed the victory over Elliott's life battle and won. Only God could have turned the situation around, what Satan meant for evil, God turned it around for good. Elizabeth's heart fluttered as gut-wrenching tears streamed down her face, and she said under her breath, *"Thank you, God."*

Catie wanted to meet her brother so badly, and the nurses would not allow her to come into the PICU. Hospital protocol. Elizabeth shared with the nurse that Catie wanted to meet her baby brother, and much to Elizabeth's surprise they moved Elliott's crib to the viewing window. Catie and Joe met Elliott through the window. The nurse asked if Catie would like a picture of Elliott to take home since she couldn't meet him face to face. Elizabeth said *"Yes, that would be very thoughtful of you,"* and to Elizabeth's surprise, she did.

144

Leaving the hospital this time, Joe, Elizabeth, and Catie's spirits were heightened more than any time before. God had fulfilled the scripture in their lives once again. He affirmed ways were always the best.

Catie placed the picture on her bedside table and kissed Elliott goodnight before saying her prayers and turning out the light. Although she was anxious to hold him, the picture seemed to satisfy the desire for now.

Elizabeth returned to the hospital the following day, and the nursing staff had moved Elliott's crib to the front window permanently so Catie could see him when she visited. Elliott had another good night and his stats continued to improve. Elizabeth was able to feed him and rock him. Holding him close and claiming the victory, her heart swelled. She thought, *"I may not have birthed you physically son, but I did spiritually."*

The nursing staffs had shared how uncomfortable they were with Elizabeth, Elliott's adoptive mom, and Cher, Elliott's birth mother, caring for him, but were willing to try to work with them. Elizabeth took care of Elliott during the day and Cher took care of him in the evening. Her dear friend Elizabeth W. had created a banner of scripture for his crib claiming victory over his life, and Elizabeth hung the banner and would read those scriptures to Elliott every day.

On Wednesday of that week, Elizabeth finally had a chance to talk to the doctor. With Elliott improving every day and a decrease in his white blood count, as well as the increase of nutrition he was able to take, his hospital stay could hopefully be coming to an end. The doctor originally had not given a discharge date for Elliott due to his critical condition upon birth. The initial prognosis wasn't encouraging, but he shared that if Elliott continued on the current path he could possibly go home by Friday, six days from his birth.

He would still need continual care in relation to the higher level of antibiotics they were administering through the PICC, but a home health care nurse would administer his dosage and management at home, as well as the maintenance of the PICC. The doctor continued to share that one of the side effects of the higher-level antibiotics Elliott was taking was the loss of hearing. Elizabeth wasn't going to accept that and thanked God right then and there, a hearing loss was not going to happen to him.

Friday came, and Elliott's homecoming was on the horizon! The hospital picture was taken in an outfit Catie and Elizabeth picked out together. It was a blue gingham print and had smocking on the front with an embroidered train set. The nurse placed a baby blue handmade knitted hat over his head, so the PICC wouldn't show for the picture. Once the discharge paperwork was executed, Cher, her mother Kathy, Joe, Elizabeth, Catie, and Elliott left the hospital. They had to stop at the adoption agency prior to going home to complete the final paperwork for the adoption.

Elizabeth had invited Cher and her mother Kathy to come to their home and place Elliott in his cradle after everything was finalized. A thunderstorm was in full force, the rain was intense and came down hard, and Joe, Elizabeth, Catie, and Elliott were soaked. Catie thought it was really funny. Once home, she changed her clothes and kept asking, *"Mommy when can I hold Elliott? Mommy, please!"* She wouldn't stop asking until she held her brother. Catie jumped up on Elizabeth and Joe's bed and Elizabeth gave Elliott to Catie. She looked at him with intensity, *"He's really my brother isn't he Mommy?"* Elizabeth stood and took pictures of her beautiful children. She wanted to freeze the moment, she got down on her knees and looked at her two children God had given her, *"Yes Catie, he really is your brother. This is the brother and son God gave us."*

Cher and Kathy stayed the afternoon, and Elizabeth's heart broke for Cher. Leaving Elliott was so difficult, they all prayed together before she and Kathy left, a sweet prayer for Elliott's life. As hard as it was for Cher to leave Elliott, Elizabeth was struggling for the time she could be home alone with just Catie and Elliott.

As the afternoon progressed to early evening Elizabeth's friend, Leisha, brought a delicious meal to celebrate Elliott's homecoming. Keily finally was able to meet Catie's brother and hold him. She told Catie she liked him, which put a big smile on Catie's face. Joe came home and they all ate dinner together. They knew how blessed they were to have their family all home together.

Elizabeth reflected, as she fed Elliott that night, how very blessed she was to have walked, what she would describe as the wilderness journey that seemed like years to complete. These last six weeks proved again and again how faithful God is. The waiting, the unknowing, the dependence on God that carried her through those excruciating painful times, there were too many to number. Stretching her beyond what she thought was possible and feeling every emotion possible was worth it.

Not being able to carry children to term, being obedient when the path didn't relate to her desire, and donating her kidney to Mike were all part of God's plan for her life. If she had not chosen to take Linda to the parole officer and be obedient to serve others as God had asked, or to continue to stand by Audrey even when Elizabeth's patience and ability was stretched time after time and continuing was harder than giving up. If she had not had the hysterectomy, she wouldn't have been able to donate her kidney because she was classified as childbearing age. God was in total control the entire time. He knew the big picture and His ways are always the best. Again, Elizabeth's obedience to God to serve and act brought the desires of her heart to fruition. Blessings are not rewards. They are the outcomes of faithfulness.

God knew Elizabeth's heart's desire was to have children, and He had Catie and Elliott planned all along. Elizabeth's heart almost burst as she reflected upon how good God was to her and how much He loved her. The lessons she had learned through the journey, God shows up every time, on time, and with whatever was needed.

She reflected on the scripture that Laurie Jackson had given her, in Isaiah 43:1-2 *"Do not be afraid, for I have ransomed you. I have called you by name; you are mine. When you go through deep waters, I will be with you. When you go through the rivers of difficulty, you will not drown. When you walk through the fire of oppression, you will not be burned up; the flames will not consume you."* when she was struggling intensely with Audrey, Catie's birth mother. Seeing that scripture come to fruition, Elizabeth knew that God had blessed her with *A Dream Come True*.

She held Elliott tightly to her chest and thanked God for the adventurous journey of becoming a parent and looked forward to life as a family of four.

--TAKE AWAY--

- God can turn situations around and does all the time.

2 Kings 4:16 "Next year at this time you will be holding a son in your arms! No my Lord! She cried. O man of God, don't deceive me and get my hopes up like that. But sure enough, the woman soon became pregnant. And at that time the following year she had a son, just as Elisha had said."

Prayer and the word of God are two powerful weapons in battle. Miracles can happen today before our very eyes just as the birth of Elizabeth's son. God took a situation that in the world's eyes didn't look possible – and made it a reality. Down to the last finite detail. It seemed the situation was not in Elizabeth's favor, but she stood unwavering in her faith, petitioned to her Lord through prayer, and trusted in God's word, and through that stance, God's glory was revealed.

You too, can experience this reality. Look to God in all things – no matter the size.

About the Author

 *A Dream Come True* is Elizabeth's first effort at writing. Born out of her own experiences, she writes transparently and with anticipation of how God comforts us through life's journey. Learning to rely on God during difficult and exhaustive seasons in her life, He continues to use her fighter mentality to instill in her not to give up, but to live in the present, and use His Word as her strongest weapon in her survival toolkit. Now an empty nester, Elizabeth still uses those same tools that God taught her back then, and they WILL work for You too!

For twenty-plus years, Elizabeth has brought a message of faith, encouragement, and hope to women in difficult situations. Her speaking career with Christian Women's Club has provided a platform to share her testimony. Captivating audiences with laughter and tears through her own experiences has been her passion as a speaker.

Speaker | Story Teller | Author - Booking Opportunities contact - **TheHowellGroupTulsa@gmail.com**

Made in the USA
Coppell, TX
04 May 2023

16436161R00095